HOW TO GET
THE
JOB
YOU WANT
IN
TOUGH TIMES

HOW TO GET THE **JOB** YOU WANT IN TOUGH TIMES

JULIANNE FOWLER

Lowell House
Los Angeles

Contemporary Books
Chicago

Library of Congress Cataloging-in-Publication Data
Fowler, Julianne.
　　How to get the job you want in tough times / Julianne Fowler.
　　　　p. cm.
　　Includes bibliographical references.
　　ISBN 1-56565-038-7
　　1. Vocational guidance.　2. Career development.　I. Title.
HF5381.F695 1991
650.14—dc20　　　　　　　　　　　　　　　　　　　　　91-17185
　　　　　　　　　　　　　　　　　　　　　　　　　　　　CIP

Copyright © 1991, 1993 by RGA Publishing Group, Inc.

All rights reserved. No part of this work may be reproduced or transmitted in any form or by any means, electronic or mechanical, including photocopying and recording, or by any information storage or retrieval system, except as may be expressly permitted by the 1976 Copyright Act or in writing by the publisher.

Requests for such permissions should be addressed to:
Lowell House
2029 Century Park East, Suite 3290
Los Angeles, CA 90067

Publisher: Jack Artenstein
Vice-President/Editor-in-Chief: Janice Gallagher
Executive Vice-President: Nick Clemente
Director of Publishing Services: Mary D. Aarons
Text Design: Brenda Leach

Manufactured in the United States of America

10 9 8 7 6 5 4 3 2 1

*To my husband, Paul, and my young sons,
Ryan and Scott, for their contributions and support.
And to my many students, clients, and workshop participants over
the last twenty years for their insight and inspiration.*

Table Of Contents

Introduction 1

PART ONE — *Laying the Groundwork*
Chapter 1 — Setting Your Career Goals 5
Chapter 2 — Targeting the Right Employer 12

PART TWO — *Your Self-Marketing Package*
Chapter 3 — The Winning Cover Letter 31
Chapter 4 — The Well-Crafted Résumé:
Tailoring Your Qualifications 49
Chapter 5 — Beyond the Basics:
Other Marketing Materials 116

PART THREE — *Go Out and Get the Job!*
Chapter 6 — Beginning Your Job Search 137
Chapter 7 — How to Have a Great Interview 146
Chapter 8 — Getting Your Foot in the Door:
An Alternative for Tough Times 177

Epilogue 181

Suggested Readings 182

INTRODUCTION

"If one advances confidently in the direction of his dreams and endeavors to live the life which he has imagined, he will meet with a success unexpected in common hours."

—*Henry David Thoreau*

FINDING THE RIGHT JOB FOR YOU

You want a job, but not just *any* job! It's got to be the one that's absolutely right for you. How do you go about finding that perfect job? And how do you distinguish yourself from all the other candidates? How do you choose among all the possible career paths and discover the one that's just right for you?

Finding the right job—the one that's both satisfying and challenging for you—takes some careful, methodical self-analysis and planning. Where do you begin? How do you know what you really want in a job? How can you develop a systematic success plan for landing the right job in these tough times?

Since 1990, it seems that tough times have become tougher. Some experts say we're suffering through the longest period of economic stagnation since the Great Depression. With unemployment hovering at about 8 percent nationally—and more than 10 percent in some areas—it's harder than ever to get the job you want. But there *are* good jobs out there. To be successful in your search, it's important to understand the forces at work in the marketplace.

By most definitions, we're no longer in a recession. In some ways the prolonged stagnation is a paradox. *BusinessWeek* reported in July 1992 that, according to standard economic theory, our 2.7 percent first-quarter growth should have created 200,000 jobs. Instead, corporate payrolls declined. Companies have been forced to downsize and reduce the layers of management within their structure. Meanwhile, millions of competitive baby boomers are trying to move up into their dream jobs in middle management. Because of the baby-boom generation, there are significantly more qualified professionals than there are places for them within the corporate structure. Those people born prior to 1946 are also part of this crowded pyramid. This squeeze is worsened by the economic imperative of companies to reduce their payrolls by eliminating middle and upper management.

When the Baby Bust generation—those born during the years of declining birth rates beginning in the mid-1960s—enters the job market, industry will be experiencing a labor shortage at the entry level. This is particularly true in technical areas such as engineering and science. So, if you are lucky enough to be in the right age group, and if you have specialized in the right field, you'll enjoy the benefits of a seller's market. Whether you are a recent graduate, an unemployed victim of downsizing, a person re-entering the job market, or a job-hopper trying to find your perfect niche, this book will help you to position yourself and prepare for success in an ever-tightening job market.

Unanticipated job loss can be devastating. In these days of corporate downsizing, even long-term, successful employees of stable Fortune 500 companies are being laid off. No company or industry is immune. Many corporations such as AT&T, Wang Laboratories, IBM, and General Motors have laid off thousands. I know how difficult it is to be unemployed because I've been in that situation. I know the paralyzing fear that strikes when you don't have much experience. I'm familiar with the pain of prolonged uncertainty. I know how it feels when you're laid off and don't know where next month's rent is coming from. How can you cope with the anxiety, financial loss, and shattered dreams of unemployment?

The first step in your job search is to practice unemployment survival strategies. When you're unemployed, it's important to remember that your job now is to find a job. This focus alone will help you structure your days and give you an added sense of control over a frustrating situation. Taking concrete steps toward your goal builds damaged self-esteem. Even if you don't find a job right away, improving your self-perception will help you deal with your situation in a more constructive way.

In planning your search, here are some useful tips for success in three essential areas: personal organization, goal setting, and preparation strategies:

1. Personal Organization. Experts agree that it's important to maintain a daily business schedule for your job of finding a job. Get up at your regular time each morning and promptly get dressed. Plan your business day as you would if you were on the job—schedule time for phone calls, follow up on correspondence, network, do research, plan special projects. Establish a job search timeline with goals and milestones. Set deadlines for yourself and stick to them as you would in any critical business commitment.

Maintaining social contacts is an often neglected practice that can be helpful during this stressful time. Don't drop out of your bowling league, softball team, or aerobics class. These activities can provide much needed social support and continuity apart from the job scene. And medical experts agree that physical activity and sports are essential in maintaining your health, both mental and physical, during times of stress.

Take a careful look at your finances and map out a survival strategy with your family. Assess your resources realistically. How much of your savings are you willing to invest in the job search process? What are your current sources of income—such as unemployment checks, spouse's and children's earnings, income from renters? What are your current monthly expenses? Which ones can be reduced or deferred? Keep in mind that some payments can be reduced without affecting your credit rating. For example, see if your doctor or department store would accept a payment of, say, $10 less than the minimum. This would be better for you than skipping payments. In the end, these reductions can add up and help increase your cash flow. Finally, look for ways to bring in more income during your job search. Every little addition, no matter how small, can help to ease the burden. Get family members involved. Consider ideas such as renting out the spare room or having your teenagers organize a garage sale or take on part-time jobs. Brainstorm with everyone and you'll be surprised what good ideas teamwork can generate.

Set aside a special work area for business in your home. If you don't have a spare room to convert to an office, any quiet corner with a table and telephone will do. Make sure that your workspace is free of clutter and other distractions such as a television.

Be sure to establish an effective system for keeping files of your job contacts and important leads. It's a good idea to keep a log book of your phone conversations. Set up a tickler system to remind yourself when to make those follow-up calls. Maintaining a file or notebook of job listings and any action you've taken on each is also a good idea. When you make your job search your full-time job, you'll generate a lot of data that need to be systematically organized for maximum effect. Potential employers will be impressed with your promptness and organization.

2. Goal Setting. Once your schedule and environment are organized, you're ready to focus on yourself, your goals, and your career direction. There are many excellent organizations that provide self-assessment career testing and counseling. This can be costly, however, and if you don't have the money to invest at the moment, you can do your own analysis. A good first step is to do an inventory assessing your strengths, weaknesses, likes, dislikes, and achievements. List at least five items under each category (for example, your strengths might include excellent sales skills and an ability to work well as part of a team). Analyzing this list will put you in touch with the most important factors for determining your career choices. You might learn, for example, that you want to work at a smaller company, or that you want to change careers entirely. This will be the foundation on which you set your goals and plan your job search strategy.

Setting realistic goals is essential to your success. Know what position you're going after. In a tough job market, it's also a good idea to have one or two backup positions in mind. For example, everyone wants to rise a notch with a new job. Your goal might be to rise from junior buyer to buyer. But when there are junior buyer positions available, an across-the-board move might be a more realistic goal. In these tough times it's important to recognize that very few of us are going to continually climb the corporate ladder. The ladder is much more crowded now, and there are fewer rungs on it. A more realistic goal might be to broaden your skills, become more versatile and be the very best in your field.

3. Preparation Strategies. Now that you've gotten yourself organized and have set your goals, it's time to prepare for your job search. Many experts agree that one of the best things you can do for yourself during this difficult time is to seek help from a support group. Some state employment offices run networking sessions and job clubs. Community and church organizations frequently sponsor groups that provide motivation, job search ideas, job listings, and networking opportunities for members. They often provide experts who can offer valuable guidance.

Next, you need to lay the groundwork. Spend time developing and maintaining a strong professional network. Contact your alumni association, college career center, sorority, or fraternity. Connect with people in your field. Learn about their experiences in the industry and opportunities in their particular area. Join professional associations and attend their meetings regularly. This will provide many opportunities to make valuable contacts and establish a reputation for yourself. At this point, you should begin developing a portfolio of your best work as well as letters of recognition you received from previous jobs.

If you can afford to do so, subscribe to the *National Business Employment Weekly*, *The Wall Street Journal*, and other trade publications that list job openings in your field. Reading these publications regularly will also keep you up-to-date on employment trends and other important business issues that you can use during your job interviews. If you can't afford to subscribe right now, these publications should be on hand at the public library. The public library can also be a tremendous source of information in your hunt for information, leads, and government postings. Some larger libraries have sections devoted specifically to the job seeker, but the best thing about your local library is that the services are free.

Once the groundwork is done, you're ready to prepare your résumé and cover letter. This should be a top priority. Keep them short and focused. Don't forget to highlight your special achievements. This will help to distinguish you from the glut of candidates. It's a good idea to get some help on your résumé and cover letter by looking at successful examples and getting feedback from a trusted colleague. Chapters 3 and 4 on cover letters and résumés include useful checklists and samples from a wide variety of industries.

The purpose of the résumé and cover letter is, of course, to get an interview. Once they have been completed and sent out to prospective employers, you'll want to begin preparing for the interview. You should devote considerable time to very thorough and careful preparation. Make up some tough questions for yourself and then rehearse your answers. Go through a best-interview/worst-interview scenario. Plan out every detail of your appearance, communication style, and body language. Rehearse with a partner, videotape the session, and critique your performance. Repeat this procedure until you're satisfied with the results. Then rehearse daily so that perfect performance comes as second nature when you're in that all-important interview. When you're unemployed, following these steps will give you a sense of control and help you cope successfully with your anxieties and financial stress. Remember, this is also a time to change direction and build new dreams. Chapter 7 contains a self-checklist and added details on interview preparation.

Preparation for the job search is important, but so is persistence and patience. There are going to be times when it seems as though nothing is going to happen, that every lead has been played out. Don't give up! That next job offer might be right around the corner. Take a long look at all your viable options and go after them. Something is bound to happen if you persist.

One good example of patience and persistence is a 49-year-old electrician named John. He was working for a medium-sized construction firm all through the 1980s, and work and overtime had been plentiful. He had just been promoted to supervisor when he got his layoff notice. John was in shock. He had felt secure working at the same firm for such a long time. Now he didn't know what to do.

He began by checking with his buddies at other construction firms around the city. Their companies were also laying off. When he went to file for unemployment, he learned about a job club run by the state Employment Development Department. At one session the instructor advised John to learn new skills and develop a marketing strategy for himself. Through networking at the job club, he found that the home remodeling segment of the industry was experiencing some growth. So he decided to make himself more marketable by taking courses at a trade tech school in carpentry and painting. John realized that even in a real estate slump, there's an ongoing need for handymen and home repair and maintenance work. If he could learn to build specialized items such as storage closets and bathroom vanities, he could market himself as a home improvement specialist.

Generally, tradesmen don't use résumés or business cards, so John didn't know how to begin this type of self-marketing. The job club counselor was able to help him out. He gave John several good ideas to get started in promoting his freelance home improvement business. As a first step he suggested that John design a colorful flier listing his capabilities, his name, and his phone number. He should also have some business cards printed up and distribute them everywhere: the lumberyard, building supply stores, the local union, door-to-door in residential areas, and even on car windshields.

It's been a year since John got laid off. With his broader skill base and energetic marketing, he's now doing fairly well. Freelance work has its advantages and disadvantages. Stability is often uncertain and work is spotty at times. But the potential for growth is unlimited and the rewards are in proportion to your efforts.

John is now back at trade school in his spare time, studying for his general contractor's license, and remains optimistic. He commented, "If I did all this in only a year, just think what I can do with my future!"

Changing Economic Times

Employers and labor unions alike remain skeptical, unsure of the new forces at work: changing trade agreements, global competition, rapid technological progress, and ubiquitous automation.

Changing Trade Agreements. Trade agreements have had a dramatic effect on the market, particularly for lower skilled workers, in a wide spectrum of industries. As trade barriers began to ease in recent years, imports began displacing low-skilled workers in many stable industries such as electronics, auto parts, and textiles. Offshore labor began replacing low-skilled back-office workers such as data entry clerks. Analysts are predicting that increased global trade will raise demand for higher skilled work. This could lead to a shortage of highly skilled workers, especially in technology-driven markets such as computers, medicine, and engineering. But where will the 30 million displaced, lower skilled workers go? Can the service sector absorb them all?

Global Competition. Because of the profound economic and social changes worldwide, many industries such as defense, financial services, energy, and aerospace are downsizing permanently. Global competition in every arena, from automobiles to electronics to textiles to aircraft, has underscored the need for selective hiring. Currently, for every open position there is a glut of qualified candidates.

Technological Change. The rapid pace of technological change in the 1990s has been lethal. To survive, companies need to become flexible and adapt readily. Wang, a dominant computer giant of the 1980s, was too large and cumbersome to adapt. While their lean competitors were able to move ahead with personal computer and microchip technology, Wang was left far behind. They filed for bankruptcy in August 1992, cutting their ranks to 8,000 from 32,000. To remain technologically competitive, successful companies are becoming smaller and more focused on service and development. This strategy requires fewer workers than in previous eras when the focus was on manufacturing and mass production. Industry giants such as IBM and Hewlett Packard have cut their ranks sharply in the past decade to keep pace with technological change. With the new emphasis on development, there are now more jobs in the high-skill areas of research and engineering.

Automation. Automation is sharply reducing the work force in almost every segment. Service industries such as finance, communication, retail, hotels, and restaurants, who currently employ 75 percent of the work force, are automating and displacing lower skilled workers. AT&T has cut 21,000 low-skill jobs since 1984, but at the same time increased white-collar hires by 8,000. *Fortune* magazine reports that 1.5 million manufacturing jobs have been lost in the United States, but it also reports the creation of more jobs than any other country. Most are in small businesses, and the number of small businesses is growing faster than any other segment of the economy. These businesses need to find well-qualified, trained, experienced workers.

Changing Marketplace and Current Trends. The changing economic environment has created a new marketplace with different employer needs. Because of downsizing and competitive pressures, employers today need workers who are highly trained, multiskilled, and flexible. There is a current trend in business to do more with less. As a result employers are looking for workers who are flexible and skilled enough to wear two hats and pick up any slack. Another result of this trend is that employees are required to work together and support one another as members of a team. This requires training for highly developed communication and interpersonal skills. This trend toward flexibility requires employees to have a "can do" attitude to do whatever it takes to get the job done—long hours, travel, and weekend work.

There's a growth trend in the small business arena. In today's economy, 75 percent of all workers are employed by small businesses. And small business continues to create more new jobs than any other segment of the economy. This has created a viable market for the prepared job seeker.

Today's job seeker needs to be aware of these trends and changes to make sure that they are positioned to take advantage of rising labor demands. Research and proper self-evaluation is important for anyone who might need to make a career change to fit these tougher economic times.

Chris, a 28-year-old software engineer was laid off from his aerospace job but his subsequent retraining helped him move on after the loss. He had worked for the same firm his entire career. When he got laid off, he realized he needed to broaden his skill base and transfer to a more growth-oriented industry. His research revealed that medicine and related industries are currently experiencing growth, along with a high demand for skilled professionals. Many experts agree that this trend is expected to continue into the next century because of rapid technological advances and the growing market based on the aging baby boomer population.

In school, Chris had always had an interest in physiology and physical education. With the downturn in education, however, he knew that teaching was not a good alternative, and becoming a doctor didn't seem practical at this point. So he began to investigate other health-care professions and found that with his background, it would take him only two years to become a licensed physical therapist. He could take a full courseload at college while freelancing as a software engineer to help finance his education. After graduation, Chris will have several career options that call for a combination of his computer skills and knowledge of physical therapy. He is currently working for a promising start-up company that develops virtual-reality software for application in sports training and therapy.

How to get better jobs in a changing marketplace

A. Strategies

Opportunity has been defined as preparation and timing. To take advantage of opportunities in new and expanding businesses, it's essential that you prepare yourself by upgrading your skills and retraining.

An important part of your job of finding a job is enhancing your qualifications. Most industry analysts agree that the current trend is moving toward a higher skilled work force. Many of the low-skill jobs have already moved offshore or been lost to automation. At every level, upgrading your skills is critical to your career success.

Even though the job search period can be filled with stress and anxiety, it can also be a time of tremendous personal growth. No longer constrained by rigorous work and travel schedules, your time is suddenly freed up to take that computer class or certificate program you've been wanting to do for so long. Training is a worthwhile investment of your hard-earned savings and will improve your job prospects and earning power in the long run. Get course catalogs from your local junior college, university extension, adult education, or trade school. Sign up for classes and continue to upgrade your skills or learn a new line of work. Often it only takes a few classes to qualify you for a good position in a new field.

Peter Drucker advises victims of corporate downsizing to go back to school and become specialists. This is the age of the specialist—computer, research, engineering. There is a great need for specialists everywhere, especially in start-up businesses. Small entrepreneurial ventures offer many career benefits to qualified job seekers, including rapid growth, upward mobility, and an opportunity to have an impact on the outcome and the bottom line. Frequently, in a large organization, our efforts are undervalued and we become the proverbial cog-in-the-wheel. In small businesses every individual contribution is noticeable and significant. This can provide a great sense of satisfaction for many workers.

In view of these changing economic patterns and prolonged tough times in the job market, the best strategy for a successful job search includes upgrading your skills, retraining, and canvassing small businesses in your field.

Carole is a 35-year-old teacher who taught elementary school in a small town just outside of Detroit for 12 years. Over the last few years she saw staff, pay, and benefits erode in her district. Each year the cuts were deeper and deeper until eventually Carole realized that she had to get out. Carole wondered where to go. What else could she do? She'd always been a teacher. With a master's in education and twelve years of experience, her training and skills were limited to the educational field.

A methodical planner by nature, Carole developed a three-part strategy with a two-year timeline. Her strategy included research, training, and networking. Through her research, Carole learned that there was a critical need in many small businesses and start-up organizations for business management skills. Her self-analysis revealed a talent for business. She also learned that a local university extension program offered an eight-course certificate in business management. Carole figured that she would take two courses per quarter and complete the certificate within a year. This would allow time for her to focus on a few skills courses in specialized areas of interest such as computers or marketing. The year would also be devoted to making those important networking contacts and following up on any leads. Carole felt that if all went as planned, at the end of two years she'd be prepared and positioned quite well for a successful transition.

After 10 months, as she neared completion of her certificate, Carole learned that the school where she taught was slated to be consolidated with another school, and most of the jobs at her school would be lost. She was unemployed. But she decided to continue with her original plan. Within two months, the owner of a small software development firm, whom she had met in the certificate courses, offered Carole a job as office manager. Planning and preparation had paid off for Carole.

Finding the right job is not an overnight process but one that must be planned in calculated steps. Resist the temptation to scan the want ads and send out your résumé in mass mailings. The market is different now than it was before, and it requires new strategies. The competition is fierce, and the need to be organized and resourceful is more important now than ever before. The more focused you are, the better your chances of finding something you enjoy doing. Sit down and analyze your strengths and weaknesses. What is it that *you* bring to a job that the other candidates can't? Identify a specific job and the type of company you are most comfortable with. Location, stability, and chance for advancement are all important considerations. Don't rest on your laurels, keep on educating yourself in new areas or hone the skills you already have. It's essential to set yourself above the competition. Establishing and utilizing networking contacts is the most effective way to find a new position. Do what you can to let people know you are looking for work.

Even though these might be the most difficult economic times of this generation, it can also be an opportunity for personal growth. The purpose of this book is to help you rise above the growing number of competing job seekers. Remember, your best strategy is to plan, plan, plan, and then go for it!

PART ONE

Laying the Groundwork

Laying the Groundwork

How do you begin your search for the job you want in tough times? There's a strong temptation to circle the exciting jobs listed in the classified ads, quickly get your résumé together, and begin scheduling interviews. That's what most people will be doing.

But the smart job seeker knows that this approach can be a formula for disaster. The key to success is planning—and your planning must begin with a methodical self analysis and goal setting process. This will help you identify the job and the type of employer that are right for you.

Chapters 1 and 2 take you step by step through this critical stage of your job search. You'll learn how to set up your Job Search Notebook, set and achieve your goals, and stay on target when identifying the right employer.

You'll meet successful job seekers who will help you by sharing their own success systems with you. This stage will lay the foundation for your future success.

CHAPTER 1

Setting Your Career Goals

"The best advice is to figure out what you really want to do and to then steadfastly work toward it, making the most of whatever you do along the way."
—G. Ray Runkhouser

Studies have shown that the most successful people in life are those who set goals. Going through life without goals is like starting a cross-country trip without a map, or a transatlantic journey without a compass. If you don't know where you're going and how you're going to get there step-by-step, you'll probably end up somewhere you don't want to be. It's important to realize that you're in control of your own destiny. You, and only you, can decide where you want to go and how you're going to get there.

Walt Disney was so right when he proclaimed, "If you can dream it, you can do it." He knew that a goal is simply a dream with a deadline. To make your dreams a reality, all you need to do is give yourself a deadline and start taking action. Where do you begin? First, it's important to realize that opportunity won't be knocking at your door. You must create it for yourself with careful planning, preparation and perseverance.

A good way to begin the planning process is to organize your job search with a systematic step-by-step plan. To get organized and stay focused in your job search, it's very helpful to set up a **Job Search Notebook** where you can keep all related materials. An 8½ by 11 three-ring binder or a computer notebook file are ideal for filing important documents, such as self-assessments and inventories, résumés and cover letters, copies of recommendations and requests, and information on employers.

As you build your notebook, you'll gain valuable insight by periodically reviewing the contents. Patterns will emerge. You'll recognize new strengths and employer preferences, and you'll get fresh ideas for tailoring your skills and experience.

An easy and practical way to set up your notebook or software file is to divide it into eight sections with labels corresponding to the chapters of this book. That way you'll have a section for each chronological phase of your job search.

Setting Goals

Targeting the Right Employer

Cover Letters

Résumés

Recommendations

Beginning the Job Search

The Interview

Getting Your Foot in the Door (Creative Career Alternatives)

Setting up your Job Search Notebook will establish a step-by-step action plan to keep you moving ahead in your job search. Accordingly, your first step will be to set your career goals. A good way to begin the goal-setting process is to think about where you want to go in your career. Then you can create your time line as illustrated in Figure 1.1, **Action Planning Sheet**, and determine what your first step should be. Then you can begin to take action immediately, moving in the direction of your goals. Taking that first action step helps build confidence, and having a plan already mapped out will motivate you to go on to the next step.

Once you've set up your Action Planning Sheet, you'll have a good handle on where you're going and what kind of job you're after. You can file your Action Planning Sheet in the Goals section of your Job Search Notebook. Once you've done a thorough job of planning, this sheet will be a valuable tool for many years to come.

If you're still not quite sure where you want to go or what you want to do, it would be a good idea to spend time researching career planning. The career center at your local college is a good place to start. Their services are usually free of charge and offer helpful aids such as interest and ability testing, counseling, and research materials.

A subcontracts manager at a large aerospace firm once told me how impressed he was when he interviewed Shawna for a senior buyer. Her goal-oriented planning had kept her career on track for over six years as she weathered recessions and layoffs. Because she had a plan and a goal, she wasn't afraid to switch companies for the sake of advancements. During the interview, this manager learned that Shawna had developed a 10-year plan (Figure 1.1) when she began her first job after college. This plan served as a guide to keep her energies focused. It worked well for Shawna as a powerful steering mechanism. After six years, Shawna had stayed pretty much on target and was more than halfway to her goal of becoming a subcontract administrator. It's important to keep in mind that things won't always go as planned (remember Murphy's Law), so the key is flexibility. It's essential that you build flexibility into your plan because flexibility is a critical component of successful planning. Give yourself a range of two to three years to achieve each goal. This is the key to successful goal setting. As Oliver Wendell Holmes stressed, "The greatest thing in the world is not so much where we stand, as in what direction we are moving."

In setting your career goals, remember that it's not always necessary to set your sights on moving into management, especially during tough times. With corporate downsizing and so many baby boomers

\multicolumn{3}{c}{**Action Planning Sheet**}
\multicolumn{3}{c}{(Shawna's Sample)}
Time	Contracts Career	Action Notes
Yr. 8 – 10	Subcontract Administrator	The next step, subcontract administrator, could occur between 8–10 years. Positioning is key here. Find a good department, boss, and mentor.
Yr. 5 – 7	Senior Buyer	In 5–7 years I'll be a senior buyer.
Yr. 3 – 4	Buyer	After spending a year or two as junior buyer I should move up to buyer. If not, change cos. again for promotion.
Yr. 1 – 2	Junior Buyer	In 1–2 years I should be promoted to junior buyer. If not, I can go to another company.
6 – 8 mos. Entry Level	Electronic Parts position as Assistant Buyer	Spend about 6–8 mos. in a systematic job search to find the perfect job for me.
Today		Begin Job Search

Figure 1.1

competing for fewer slots on the corporate ladder, fast tracking can be an unrealistic goal. Because of this, in recent years there's been a tremendous boom in consulting, free-lancing, job shopping, franchising, and entrepreneuring as baby boomers seek creative alternatives to the corporate climb. As part of your long-range career plan, you may want to pursue one or more of these options as a sideline as a tough times safety net. Some entrepreneurial options such as consulting, free-lancing, and job shopping can be used to establish credibility and get your foot in the door. This will be discussed in more detail in Chapter 8.

For now, remember to incorporate creativity and flexibility into your career planning.

SUCCESS ENHANCER

You can learn a great deal about career building from successful people in your chosen field. Talk to as many successful people at courses and professional associations as you can. Learn how they carved out a career niche in their field and worked their way up. We'll discuss other networking possibilities in later chapters.

Many such people can give you ideas for capitalizing on your specialized knowledge. These conversations will get your career planning ideas working.

Extension course instructors can be a valuable resource in learning about a new field. For example, if you're taking an advertising class, chances are that your instructor is an experienced professional in that field who would be more than happy to share his or her expertise with you. This is an excellent way for you to learn the ins and outs of the business.

Extension courses, learning centers, and junior colleges in most communities are usually very reasonably priced, and they're available to everyone. It's a great way to get your job search started on the right track. Attending professional society meetings and trade conferences can provide you with the opportunity to network with successful people, get ideas for your search, and make valuable connections.

For many individuals, moving up in their specialization is the right goal. Craig, a software engineer I've known for many years, established career goals within his area of expertise. When he started with a small systems development company 10 years ago, he decided that he wanted to move up from a salary grade 2 to salary grade 9–11 within 10 years. After 10 years, he's made it to a grade 9 and feels pleased. With a flexible goal, Craig was able to achieve success.

Career goals don't necessarily have to be linear or geared toward upward mobility. Many individuals find greater satisfaction in developing a breadth of knowledge in their field. Scientists, researchers, and technical experts, for instance, often prefer to branch out into related areas rather than progressing up the management ladder. If this approach appeals to you, you can establish your career goals accordingly.

One of my employees, Helen, is a very successful human resources expert who decided while she was in college that she wanted to gain experience in every area of human resources. Consequently, during the last decade, she's become very knowledgeable in staffing, training, compensation and benefits, labor relations, and communication. She's held responsible jobs in each of these areas and is now uniquely positioned for advancement.

You will eventually find the right job—it's out there. You need to be creative, and you need to be patient. In Chapter 2, "Targeting the Right Employer," we'll talk more about how to find the right fit. For now, it's sufficient to identify your preferences in the area of job structure. This knowledge can be turned into a focused strength that will work for you.

Identifying your strengths as they relate to job structure is critical to finding a job that's the right fit for you. You'll need to explore issues such as the following **Job Structure Preferences**. File your answers to these questions in the first section of your Job Search Notebook.

- Do I like to work alone or with others?
- Do I prefer variety or conformity?
- Do I like clear direction on everything, or do I like to experiment and make my own way?
- Do I enjoy relating to a lot of different people or do I prefer working with only a few?
- Do I prefer communicating by phone or in writing?
- What did I like best about previous jobs?
- Do I need to receive a lot of feedback on my work?
- Do I need to see concrete results?
- Do I prefer to follow projects through from conception to completion?

Do I prefer to work on the planning phase and then turn projects over to someone else for implementation?

Do I enjoy working with detail?

A mistake made by many people is deciding too quickly on a position that meets only their basic requirements. To avoid this and find the job that's really right for you, it's a good idea to think about your dislikes in a job situation. If the job is in a highly structured environment that requires prescriptive instructions on everything and you've always felt more comfortable in a job that requires a lot of independent problem solving, decision making, and experimentation without much direction, you're going to be unhappy. Take stock of the work (or school) situations where you were most unhappy. This will provide valuable insight and help you avoid choosing the wrong job.

SUCCESS ENHANCER

There are many excellent magazines on the market featuring success stories in every field. Go to the bookstore or library and browse; find a magazine you like and subscribe to it.

Study your industry and learn who the current heroes are. Read up on their achievements. In most cases, these are self-made individuals who can provide you with valuable advice about overcoming difficulties and reaching goals.

You've got to make your own success. Focus your strengths, set your goals, and go for it. Football coach Vince Lombardi's description of football is applicable to job and career success as well: "It's a game of inches!"

Once you've firmly established your goals, you must keep them constantly in mind. Here are two suggestion for doing this:

1. Outline your goals and post them in a place where you'll see them every day (for example, the bathroom mirror, the closet door, or the dashboard of your car). If you want to keep this private, the inside cover of a daily planner is an ideal place to post your goals.

2. Mentally picture yourself as having already achieved the next step on your goal chart. Go through this mental rehearsal every day. Before falling asleep or during exercise are good times to do this, since your mind is relaxed and very receptive at these times.

High achievers have perfected the skill of mental rehearsal. They know that if you really believe in yourself and your goals, your visualization will become reality. With daily mental rehearsal, you'll be so convinced of reaching your goals that your mind will take you there on automatic pilot. Once you decide you want to do something and visualize yourself as a success, opportunities will pop up everywhere. As Emerson said, "You become what you think about most of the time."

If you find yourself in a holding pattern, whether by choice or by circumstance, don't allow yourself to feel like a failure or to dwell on obstacles. Keep rehearsing success and never lose sight of your goals. Keep seeing yourself already there. Make adjustments and set new, achievable goals. You will get there! I *know* it can be done because I've done it myself. I changed careers, added entrepreneurial sidelines, took time out, had two babies, and nearly doubled my income three times in ten years. But to achieve these goals I overcame some tough obstacles: layoffs, unemployment, rejection, being passed over for promotion, failed ventures.

Each time I encountered setbacks, I continued to adjust my goals accordingly. Because I was able to set new goals and begin working toward them immediately, there was no time to feel like a failure. When you're moving in the direction of your goals, you're always a success. It's important to remember that success isn't a destination, it's a journey. You should enjoy every step of the way and never, ever give up. No matter what, always keep working toward your goals and you'll be a success!

Harold Melchert once said: "Live your life each day as you would climb a mountain. An occasional glance toward the summit keeps the goal in mind, but many beautiful scenes are to be observed from each new vantage point. Climb slowly, steadily, enjoying each passing moment; and the view from the summit will serve as a fitting climax for the journey."

As you take the first steps in your job search and complete this chapter on Setting Your Career Goals, you will have set up your **Job Search Notebook** and filed the following items under the first section:

Action Planning Sheet

Job Structure Preferences

CHAPTER 2

Targeting the Right Employer

"Imagination is more important than knowledge."

—*Albert Einstein*

Having defined your career goals, your next step will be to define, in a very broad sense, the type of employment which will meet your job needs. Will it be in:

    private industry

    non-profit organizations

    government

    academia

    small business

    Fortune 500 company

Which type of organization will fit your job needs and career goals identified in Chapter 1? Most people will gravitate toward the right fit based on previous experience or intuition. If you'd like to learn more about these different types of organizations, a list of excellent reference materials is included later in this chapter.

Sometimes targeting the right employer can be as simple as listing your likes and dislikes in a job situation, and then seeking an employer who offers most of your likes with a minimum of dislikes. This method worked well for Ann, a recent grad, who was thoroughly dazzled by all the choices. She had studied marketing and many of her colleagues were going for jobs with the glamour corporations. One colleague was encouraging her to join a small but successful consulting group, while another thought she'd be happier doing freelance work and striking out on her own. By listing a few of her important likes and dislikes, the right choice quickly emerged (see

Figure 2.1). After talking with colleagues who had joined large agencies, Ann knew their jobs were very structured and really controlled in many areas. You can prepare your own Personal Inventory and file it in your Job Search Notebook under section 2.

Ann's Personal Inventory	
<u>Likes</u> • flexibility • variety • self-expression • working with people • being part of a group • travel • feedback • instructions that leave room for experimentation	<u>Dislikes</u> • rigidity • restrictive rules • lots of direction • too much structure • paperwork • very detailed instructions • working in isolation • working late

Figure 2.1

Ann knew that agency workers were often expected to work late hours. And free-lance work was out because she felt a strong need to work with others rather than in isolation. So, the clear choice was the small consulting group where Ann has since developed a successful career during the last five years.

IDENTIFYING THE RIGHT EMPLOYER

How would you describe your ideal employer? You'll probably say this would be a company that is people oriented and that offers job security, generous benefits, and growth opportunities. These characteristics sound good, but what do they really mean? What does a people-oriented company look like and act like? How do you know whether a company is stable, and whether it really will provide you with the growth opportunities promised in the interview?

Matching your needs with an employer's style is critical in finding the right job. Understanding corporate personality can mean the difference between finding the perfect job and one that will make you miserable. You've got to do some research and ferret out the clues that will lead to a great match.

You may have a strong temptation to skip this step and take the first reasonable offer. As with relationships, there is frequently a tendency toward "love at first sight," falling for good looks and charm. This happened to me when I was looking for my first job, fresh out of graduate school, with my Communications M.A. in hand. During my search, I was so dazzled by all the wrong things that I settled for a dead-end job as a "research assistant," which I later learned was nothing more than a euphemism for a receptionist position in which I was "allowed" to file research materials!

What was it that impressed me so much about this company? How could I, an intelligent, educated person, get sucked into such a trap? In a nutshell, it was looks and charm. The company was located in a spacious, new, high-rise building with a prestigious downtown L.A. address. The offices were elegantly designed and appointed with plush furniture and glamorous prints. Everyone who worked there seemed cool and confident. I decided immediately that this place was definitely better than those other bare-bones, hustle-bustle offices where I'd interviewed.

In spite of my naivete, I did manage to check out some of the right things about this company. I asked about upward mobility and was told that after six months all the "girls" (that should have been my first clue—even in 1973, "girls" was a demeaning term!) got promoted to sales assistant and moved up from there. That sounded just great to my novice ears. So I neglected to ask several important questions:

- What exactly does a sales assistant do?
- What exactly is the salary increase?
- What's the career path after sales assistant?
- How many women have been promoted to higher levels in the last two years?
- How many female managers are there in the firm?

When I asked about benefits, I was impressed that the company provided theater and ballgame tickets for employees. Later, I learned that these were only available on a last-minute basis when clients were unable to use them.

I thought the company was people-oriented because they had a beautiful employee lounge. What I didn't find out was that the managers had an even more gorgeous lounge upstairs, and that part of my duties would be to make their coffee and order their refreshments.

It's an easy trap to fall into. How can you uncover the truth before it's too late and avoid falling for the wrong company and the wrong job? The answer is in two parts:

1. Know exactly what you want.
2. Know how to get information on potential employers.

Let's take each point separately.

Identifying Exactly What You Want

Your clear career goals, established in Chapter 1, will be the most important basis for targeting employers. When I was going through a career change (from teaching to business) I started by brainstorming what I really wanted in a career and an employer. I came up with an employer profile of 25 specific items (see Figure 2.2). I found that it helps to prioritize the items, using a simple system such as the headings "must have" and "flexible." That way, you're not locking yourself into something that's unrealistically rigid. You need to allow room for that "gut feeling," which is really just reliable intuition based on experience. Discounting your feelings about any decision can be a real mistake, because feelings are a very important factor. The key, though, is to balance feelings with objective facts.

Developing an **Employer Profile Worksheet** (to be kept in your Job Search Notebook under section 2) will help you to find—and keep—that balance between objectivity and emotion. Figure 2.3 shows the employer profile worksheet prepared by Jack, a budget analyst who came to me for help in evaluating potential employers. In setting up your own employer profile, take time to think it through. Be creative. Go back to your worst job ever, as I did, so that you can learn from your mistakes. What were the significant areas that made you hate that job? What questions can you ask an employer to evaluate those areas that are important to you?

Then go through and list your priorities by placing them in categories, as Jack did (Figure 2.3). I recommend no more than two or three categories, as anything more than that can become self-defeating in its complexity. Figure 2.4 provides a blank worksheet for you to copy and use for your analysis.

Once you've rated your priorities by placing a ✔ in the appropriate column, you can list prospective employers at the bottom and evaluate them by totaling the number of "must haves" and "flexibles" you've checked off. Leave a final column for special comments that might be helpful in your decision making or for adding particular strong points which might offset other weaknesses.

With your worksheet completed on several employers, you're

ready to do a comparative analysis so you can target your top prospects. The Employer Profile Worksheet worked well for Jack when he was torn between two jobs and two very different employers.

Both potential jobs had appealing features. Once Jack outlined and prioritized his needs on the Employer Profile Worksheet, his choice became clear.

Detailed techniques for comparing two companies and two jobs

Employer Profile Sample Items

not more than 30 minute commute .... M
opportunity for advancement .... M
excellent health insurance .... M
savings plan .... M
job security .... M
growth company .... M
variety of job options .... M
work with lots of people .... M
no overtime requirements .... M
regular day shift hours .... M
limited business travel .... M
paid vacation .... M
paid sick leave .... M
retirement plan .... M
training opportunities .... M
annual raise .... M
dental plan .... F
vision plan .... F
child care .... F
recreation center .... F
educational reimbursement .... F
starting salary increase 10% .... F
size of company .... F
credit union .... F
public transportation .... F

M = *Must Have*
F = *Flexible*

Figure 2.2

Employer Profile Worksheet
(Jack's sample)

Desired Employer Characteristics	Must Have	Flexible	Comments
Company & Work Conditions			
Advancement Opportunity	✓		well-defined career track
Starting salary increase 10%	✓		
Variety in work	✓		
Few travel assignments	✓		travel rarely required
Company fiscal health	✓		
Flextime		✓	
Company size		✓	
Benefits:			
Excellent health insurance	✓		50/50 Rx 80/20 medical
Dental plan		✓	
Vision Plan		✓	
Retirement	✓		
Bonus Plan	✓		Annual
Paid Vacation	✓		2 weeks
Other:			
Commute under 30 minutes	✓		
Free Parking		✓	
Safe Location		✓	
Training Opportunity	✓		
Educational Reimbursement	✓		
Overtime		✓	Some late nights and weekends required with pay
Company growth		✓	
Employer Name: ABC Assoc.			
Total:	12	8	

Figure 2.3

will be discussed in Section Three of this book. While this may seem to be putting the cart before the horse, it's important to have your employer match in mind before creating your self-marketing package.

Obtaining Information about Potential Employers

There are many excellent, reliable sources of information on publicly held companies. Most organizations have a public relations director who will be happy to send you free information about the

Employer Profile Worksheet (blank form)			
Desired Employer Characteristics	Must Have	Flexible	Comments
Job Characteristics			
Benefits			
Other			
Employer Name:			
Total:			

Figure 2.4
You can make several copies of this blank form for your notebook, filling in your own particulars. When you begin your job search, you can use these worksheets to evaluate each prospective employer and to compare different companies based on interviews and other information. More specifics on how to get information about the job and the employer will be discussed in the following pages.

company and their products. It's well worth a phone call. Annual reports and promotional brochures will tell you a lot about a firm and help answer your questions regarding financial soundness, annual sales, and profitability. Such careful analysis of the firm's stability is particularly important during tough economic times. This literature will provide clues to the corporate culture. For example, do they emphasize the team or the individual? What do they say (or not say) about employee benefits and growth opportunities? If the offices are plush, be skeptical. Such amenities could be taking money from employee salaries and benefits!

Other excellent reference materials can be found in:

- your local library (ask librarian for help)
- local bookstores (business or reference section)
- *The Wall Street Journal*
- other business publications
- trade journals
- trade associations
- job fairs
- university career centers
- business section of daily newspapers
- *100 Best Companies to Work For* (and other such books)
- university bookstores
- *Dun and Bradstreet* ratings

Once you've done your basic research, you'll be able to evaluate each employer on many of the characteristics on the Employer Profile Worksheet. To fill in the ones you've missed, you'll need to do some additional research. Talk to people who work at a company you're interested in. Professional Associations provide a good way to contact others in your profession. These societies usually publish annual directories listing members, their employers, titles, and phone numbers. When you call saying that your professional society referred you to them for advice, most members will be happy to help. Ask how they feel about their jobs, their growth opportunities, or whatever's important to you. Try calling the general number at the front office. It's surprising how much can you can learn from the receptionist's attitude. If she seems rude and harried, that's a clue. She may be overworked, underpaid, and miserable. Does she lack basic training in communication skills and customer relations? Companies who truly care about their people and their customers will give top priority to the receptionist function.

Although the source may be a bit biased, talking to the competition can be an excellent way to learn about a prospective employer. Does the company have a reputation for ruthless layoffs, autocratic management, questionable ethics? Of course, you can't believe everything you hear, but if you talk to enough people, solid patterns will begin to emerge. Trade associations, alumni associations, and professional societies offer excellent opportunities for sharing information about employers.

Once you've sized up potential employers to see whether they match your Employer Profile, the next step is to get out there and market yourself to them.

How—And Where—To Find Employers

In these tough, competitive times, simply filling out an application or sending in a résumé won't be enough. You've got to be creative and persistent. Often, the best way to do this is to seek employers in several different ways. If you keep at it, sooner or later you'll find the right match. The following are the most common ways to find employers:

- employment agencies
- executive recruiter
- professional recruiter
- yellow pages—cold calling
- classifieds
- walk-in
- direct mail campaign
- campus interview
- company recruiter
- professional association
- college placement office
- job/trade fair
- job shop agency
- networking

In the next paragraphs, we'll look at each of these in turn.

Employment Agencies

Employers who don't want to deal with the general public retain agencies to pre-screen applicants for specific qualifications. The agency then refers applicants to the employer for interview and evaluation. You can find these agencies in the yellow pages under "Employment." Some agencies specialize in recruiting for a specific industry, such as accounting, entertainment, management, or finance.

Advantages – Employment agencies can usually land you a job quickly. You need to analyze the job and employer (Employer Profile Worksheet) to make sure it's the right job for you. Agencies build your confidence and make the job sound perfect for you. I know many who have used this method to successfully land several jobs in various fields that worked out very well.

Disadvantages – You may be required to pay a fee which can be a significant percentage of your salary for a specified period of time. But to land the right job in tough times it could be well worth the fee.

Executive/Professional Recruiter

Executive/professional recruiters (more commonly known as headhunters) usually have excellent, well-placed connections and know about openings which are not made public. I used a headhunter once when I was discouraged by the dismal prospects and needed a job right away. But the company wasn't right for me and I left after only six months. On the other hand, my colleague Bob landed several excellent advertising management positions at both large and small companies through headhunters. Many recruiting firms specialize in specific areas, such as administrative, financial, managerial and technical. These are listed in the yellow pages under "Employment."

Advantages – Headhunters keep their fingers on the pulse of the industry. They're alert to trends and know where to look.

Disadvantages – You may be required to pay a substantial fee. Headhunters will sometimes use the "hard sell" approach and railroad you or the employer into something you're not quite sure of. So, beware!

Campus Interview

Campus career planning centers routinely set up career day recruiting interviews with local companies. It's a good idea for juniors and seniors to stay in touch with the career planning center and keep alert to interview opportunities. Try to go to as many interviews as possible for exposure and practice.

Advantages – Most career planning centers offer interview coaching sessions which can be very helpful. Going to a number of interviews will help you identify what's important to local employers in your field so that you can tailor your self-presentation accordingly. It will also help you learn more about what your options are.

Disadvantages – Many employers who participate in campus interviews are evaluating candidates on extremely narrow criteria (such as GPA). They erroneously believe that they're recruiting the highest potential employees by seeking only top students. Follow-up studies have proven that this is a recruiting mistake because the best employees are often the "B" and "C" students who exhibit leadership and people skills through participation in extracurricular activities, team sports, and part-time employment. Campus interviewers are often blind to this, while many corporate interviewers tend to evaluate on broader criteria.

SUCCESS ENHANCER

Ask other people to tell you about their best and worst jobs ever. Pay particular attention to issues that involve complaints such as these: "The job wasn't at all what I thought it would be!" or "It wasn't anything like the job description!" Ask the person what he or she would do differently to avoid such problems in the future.

After you've conducted best job/worst job interviews with between five and ten people, you will notice certain patterns emerging that will help you to draw conclusions about what to look for in an employer. File this information in your Job Search Notebook under section 2, and refer to it often.

Company Recruiter

Large companies frequently retain professional recruiters to assist managers in finding qualified candidates for openings in their departments.

Advantages – Recruiters have a difficult seek-and-find-mission, so they often welcome unsolicited applicants. Don't be afraid to call a company and ask to speak to the recruiter in your area. You could be the candidate of their dreams and save them a lot of leg work.

Disadvantages – Recruiters say that managers often give them impossible requirements to fill. Managers are looking for someone who walks on water. Then when they find that person, he's also got to part the Red Sea! This can be a tough bill for candidates to fill. But if you impress the recruiter, he or she can often sell you to the hiring manager.

Professional Associations

Frequently professional associations will maintain listings of job opportunities. Some will even provide a referral service for employers looking for talent. All you need to do is register with the association and they'll give your name to employers who call requesting someone with your background. College placement offices also operate like this. So, it's a good idea to register with as many offices as possible to maximize your exposure.

Advantages – This is just one more strategy in your career plan. It won't be your only move so you've got to use it in concert with other strategies as a sort of backup plan. The advantage is that it gives you visibility with a broad range of employers whom you may not be able to contact otherwise. This strategy came through and got a college teaching position for Pat, a program director of a large university. During the glut of the late seventies, college faculty positions were virtually nonexistent for those without college teaching experience, so Pat was caught in the proverbial "Catch 22." After what seemed an eternity for her (five years of high school teaching), the community college professional association she'd registered with gave her name to one of the colleges that needed someone on the spur of the moment...bingo, she was in. Suddenly, she'd reached her goal of college instructor. Five years of persistence in filling out those forms to reregister with the college referral association had finally paid off!

Disadvantages – Registering with an association or placement office can be a little like filing with the state unemployment office in that you're one among a cast of thousands with no opportunity to distinguish yourself. Often the bureaucratic process is cumbersome and inefficient. Some employers will only check with these offices as a last resort because they reason that any candidate with anything on the ball and even the least bit of initiative will use a more aggressive job search strategy. (That's why you're using this strategy in concert with several others.) But every once in a while the system works for you and can lead to the right job—even in tough times.

Job Fairs and Trade Fairs

These events are usually sponsored by civic organizations and industry groups and they're held at local convention centers or hotels.

Advantages – At these events you'll have the opportunity to check with many employers at the same time. You can compare their qualifications all in one day and get a good feel for what's going on in your industry.

Disadvantages – Frequently these fairs have a high-powered sales orientation which can leave job seekers feeling somewhat overwhelmed. Some vendors will be pushing their products as well as recruiting candidates. For the discriminating applicant, though, this can be an interesting way to compare companies and learn about their products. Blake, one of my career workshop participants, landed his job as a computer salesman for a large firm this way. He said it worked like a charm!

Job Shops

Sometimes referred to as temporary agencies, job shops operate much like employment agencies. Employers pay the agency a fee for providing qualified professionals for temporary positions. Temporary can mean anything from a few hours to an indefinite timeframe, sometimes extending for years. You work for the agency and are paid by them on a weekly basis.

Advantages – Job shopping is an excellent way for you to check out an employer from the inside. You can learn all about the company and evaluate them on your Employer Profile Worksheet. If you like the company and want to hire on permanently, you have the added advantage of being a known entity, which gives you a definite edge over any outside competition. Often the pay at job shop agencies is higher (because there are no benefit packages). As the cost of benefit plans escalates, employers are relying more and more on outside agencies for staffing. Agencies absorb the cost of screening and testing, payroll, workers compensation insurance, and many other costly personnel functions, which makes this an attractive alternative for employers. If you don't like the company the agency sends you to, all you need to do is request a new assignment and they'll send you somewhere else. That way you don't look like a malcontent job hopper because your employer (the agency) remains constant. So, job shopping literally gives you a chance to "shop around." Nan, a proposal specialist, got her start this way. She agrees that being a job shopper is a trade-off in many ways, but it does provide opportunity in tough times.

Disadvantages – When there are corporate cutbacks, job shoppers are usually the first to be let go. As a job shopper, you won't be eligible for corporate benefits/retirement and paid vacations, although many job shop companies are now offering their own plans to attract more candidates.

Networking

This is by far the best way to find the right employer. Studies have shown that this strategy wins the most positions simply because employers would rather work with someone they know or someone who's recommended by a colleague. So, if you have access to networks, make that your key strategy and concentrate most of your energy on those contracts.

If you don't have access to any networks, you need to develop some of your own.

Advantages – Networking can connect you with openings that you may not have otherwise heard about. It will also put you in touch with people who might be able to help you in other ways such as giving you inside information about salaries, politics, and how to play the game in your field.

Disadvantages – Networking is a time-consuming process and it can take awhile before producing results. Be careful not to come on too strong. Sincerity and caring about the other person are a must. It's also a two-way street, so you need to be prepared to help others in your network by sharing information and doing favors. This will build bridges for you—someone who's indebted to you will be inclined to go out of his way to return the favor when you need something.

Networking is a critical key to your success in business. If you haven't yet developed a network, you need to begin developing your network now. If you've already established a good network, these steps will help you strengthen and build on what you already have.

1. *Make a list of contacts.* List everyone you know who could be helpful: teachers, colleagues, former bosses, friends, coaches, college pals, fraternity or sorority contacts, neighbors, relatives. File this list in your Job Search Notebook under the second section on Targeting the Right Employer. Add to the list

as you meet new contacts and you'll have a solid network, Later, as the list grows, you might want to transfer it to your word processor for easy update.

2. *Volunteer.* Joining civic or church groups is an excellent way to meet talented professionals from every field As you work together on projects and mutual goals, you'll develop valuable sources of information.

3. *Talk to people everywhere you go.* Let everyone around you know about your job search. It's surprising how many people know other people who are in a position to help you. When my job search client, Steve, was switching careers from teaching computer science to selling software, he used this one effectively. Because he was determined not to be like the teachers who sat in the faculty lounge year after year complaining about the perils of teaching and never doing anything about it, he was determined to succeed. He was so fired up about his mission that he talked about it constantly.

After putting his plan together he went after his goals relentlessly and told everyone what he was doing. When Steve met his colleague's boss at the management association, they started talking and Steve's story came out.

When the boss heard about Steve's goals, he said he knew someone at another division within his company who could really use Steve's talents. Steve got the job and it was perfect for him. After months of talking it up everywhere, this confirmed his belief that it pays to speak up (especially when you're looking for a job!).

4. *Join alumni associations and professional associations.* This is another good way to meet talented professionals from every field. In these organizations you have the added advantage of a common bond with your school or your industry. People in these groups are usually quite amiable and interested in sharing information, so you'll make valuable contacts.

5. *Volunteer for Program Committee Chairperson.* This will give you the opportunity to contact prominent speakers in your field to set up your programs. Once you've made contact, you can build a mutually beneficial relationship which could help your self-marketing.

6. *Take classes.* This is a good way to keep your skills current and meet other people in your field who are interested in self-

improvement. You'll meet people from many backgrounds and have an excellent opportunity to share ideas.

Now that you've prepared yourself for a successful job search by setting your career goals and targeting the right employer, you're ready to start presenting yourself. Part Two is full of self-marketing strategies to put you way ahead of the crowd.

As you finish this chapter on Targeting the Right Employer, you will have completed the following documents and filed them in your **Job Search Notebook.**

Personal Inventory

Employer Profile Worksheet

Results of Best Job/Worst Job Interviews

Part Two

Your Self-Marketing Package

Your Self-Marketing Package

How do you set yourself apart from the other candidates? There's more to a job search than sending out a résumé and cover letter (although these are, of course, very important; in Chapters 3 and 4 you'll learn more about such important items). Those are the basics, and everyone will be doing that. To distinguish yourself you've got to be imaginative, using techniques others may not have thought of.

Before you start contacting employers, it's critical that you carefully plan your self-marketing strategy. Following a few basic steps will put you head and shoulders above the competition. In this section you'll meet other job seekers who will share their self-marketing strategies and tell what did, and did not, work for them. They'll share letters and résumés that they've written and received. The samples included in this section are real-world letters written and received by me and my associates (identifying information has been changed to protect the writers' privacy).

During this middle phase of your job search, perseverance and imagination are the keys to success. A. L. Williams, insurance mogul and self-made millionaire, gives the following good advice in his autobiography **When All You Can Do Is All You Can Do Is Enough!**, *"Don't wait for your ship to come in; swim out to it!"*

CHAPTER 3

The Winning Cover Letter

"It's not enough to have great qualities; you should also have the management of them"

—*Francois de la Rochefoucauld*

The purpose of your cover letter is to get the employer's attention: it should introduce you, highlight your unique qualifications, make you look perfect for the job, and get your résumé read. Accordingly, it must be tailored to the specific situation and job requirements. Writing your cover letter before you write your résumé will help you to organize your skills and experience for the particular focus needed.

How can you convey to a potential employer that you're just right for a position if you're unclear about the details of the job description? This chapter provides analysis techniques for every situation along with checklists, mistakes to avoid, and solutions used by many successful job seekers.

The first step in writing your cover letter must be careful planning. Although your letter will be very short (two or three paragraphs) this letter is more than just an afterthought. It can really be the key to your success. Your planning should include two steps:

Matching your talents to the job description.

Outlining what you want to say.

MATCHING YOUR TALENTS TO THE JOB DESCRIPTION

This is the secret to making yourself sound perfect for the job. Naturally, you'll want to find out as much as you can about the job—going beyond the job description or ad if you can.

Figure 3.0 shows some sample job ads with notes on particular points you'll want to clarify and research.

Artist/Designer Large home furnishings co. Seeks staff artist capable of designing silkscreened or embroidered kitchen towels. Background in gift, stationery or textile industry pref'd.	**Property Management Leasing Supervisor** Strong sales & administrative skills to direct large on-site sales staff. Above average salary & benefits.
1. Will this artist work alone or as part of a team? 2. Will this artist have other design responsibilities? 3. Will this artist interface with internal customers and respond to their requests? 4. Will this artist have other duties in the department? 5. To whom does this position report?	1. To whom does this supervisor report? 2. How many subordinates report to this supervisor? 3. Are subordinates all sales personnel? 4. What was annual sales of the department last year? 5. Why is this position open? 6. What kind of property does this firm lease?

Figure 3.0

Try calling and asking the manager or the representative about specific duties of the position to determine what skills or qualifications may be emphasized between the lines. Often company policy requires that the job description be written in a very general way. At the same time, the hiring manager may have quite specific criteria in mind. It's worth a call to try to find out what the hidden agenda is. This can be done in a courteous, professional conversation without appearing overly aggressive.

To record your findings, you can create a **Matching Qualifications Worksheet**. Figure 3.1 is the worksheet created by Brian.

Brian was responding to a classified ad in the *Sunday Times* placed by a large Fortune 500 high tech company where I managed a small department. At the top, he listed job requirements from the ad. Then, he called the company and spoke to a staffing representative who gave him some valuable background on special emphasis areas for the position which he listed on the worksheet. He divided the sheet into three columns, labeled as shown in the figure. At the top of column A, Brian listed the basic job requirements as they appeared in the ad or job description. (If you don't have this right now, you can conjecture what you think are the requirements of the job you want.) At the bottom of this column he listed special emphasis requirements gleaned from his phone call. Column B will be labeled "My Qualifications" and Column C, "Outline for Cover Letter."

In column B, Brian listed his qualifications and matched them to job requirements from the ad and phone call in column A. In Brian's case, his qualifications were a perfect fit for the job requirements, so he knew this was the right job for him. You may find yourself in a situation where your qualifications are not an exact match; but you still want the job. Sometimes this will work, if, for example, the employer isn't really set on his or her requirements. Often there's flexibility in the position, so you'll need to sell yourself to show that you are right for the job. Highlight what you have to offer, and downplay any areas where you come up short.

If the hiring manager isn't available when you call, ask if there is someone else you can talk to about the position. Often the hiring manager delegates applicant screening to a recruiter or staff member who will be glad to help you. In most cases, this person will be more than willing to answer your inquiries. Ask such questions as:

> How did this position become vacant?
>
> Will this person be working independently or as part of a team?
>
> What level of management does this position report to?
>
> What is the primary responsibility of this position?
>
> Do they have any special projects waiting in the wings for the candidate?

When you establish rapport with the speaker it's often surprising how much they'll tell you, so ask about anything that's important to you.

Answers to these questions can provide valuable clues to specific job requirements. For example, you might learn that in addition to technical skills and experience requirements they're looking for someone with highly developed people skills and diplomacy to smooth out particular personnel conflicts or that they need someone with crisis management skills to put out fires. With this information, you can write your cover letter emphasizing your exceptional human relations skill and ability to work well under pressure. This will give you

A Job Requirements	B My Qualifications	C Outline for Cover Letter
Master's Degree in Human Resources or related field (from ad)	**MBA, Human Resources** (not needed in cover letter—included on résumé)	**Introduction/ Position Sought** Human Resources Specialist ad in Sunday Times
6 Years Experience (from ad) human resources development organizational development related field	**10 Years Experience** human resources development organizational development	**Why Applying** perfect match **Qualifications** (from Column B) program design/delivery group facilitation needs analysis organizational planning corporate setting
Special Emphasis (from phone call) program design presentation skill group facilitation needs analysis organizational planning work with corporate managers people skills	**Special Emphasis** program design presentation skill group facilitation needs analysis organizational planning work with corporate managers people skills	**Benefit to Firm** energy commitment **Next Step** request meeting with them give my phone number

Figure 3.1: Matching Qualifications Worksheet, Brian's sample

a definite edge over candidates who point out only their technical skills.

What if you're unable to contact anyone at the firm? This happens sometimes, particularly with a blind ad. And there's not much you can do about it. Just make the most of what information you do have. Be sure to analyze the requirements carefully. If possible, talk to people in the industry (those you've met through networking) who might be able to give you some inside information to help you read between the lines.

When you have a good idea of what the job needs are, you're ready to assess your unique qualifications. The best way to get started on this is to go to your Job Search Notebook (sections 1 and 2) and review these items:

Action Planning Sheet

Job Structure Preferences

Personal Inventory

From these items you can select your special abilities and needs that match the job. Add your education and experience and record these on your Matching Qualifications Worksheet (Figure 3.1) in column B. (This information should parallel the job requirements in column A.)

The Matching Qualifications Worksheet will also help you to recognize when the job really isn't right for you. Sometimes an ad will sound so good—full of glittering enticements. But when you begin to analyze the job requirements and match them with your qualifications, you find there's not much of a match.

Notice that in column C of his Matching Qualifications Worksheet, Brian only mentions special emphasis areas, which he learned from his phone call to the employer. This is what makes him sound perfect for the position. Basic job requirements from the ad (degree and years of experience) need not be mentioned, because Brian has included them prominently in his résumé.

Be selective, highlighting only those items that will enhance your qualifications regarding this particular job. For example, when Scott applied for the position of automotive engineer, it made sense for him to highlight the fact that he'd built an award-winning hot rod. However proud you are of other accomplishments, don't include them if they're not relevant to the job. Sheila made this mistake in her cover letter applying for a consumer research job: "I'm also good at rock climbing and square dancing." This would have a negative effect on any employer who has a bias against these types of activities.

Highlight your special abilities and accomplishments that supplement your technical ability and will contribute significantly to your success on the job. List these on a sheet to be filed in your Job Search Notebook for future reference. Frequently, these traits will score more points than skill or experience alone, because getting the job done almost always depends heavily on qualities such as:

diplomacy

perseverance

communication

problem solving

It pays to make this an important focus in your cover letter because it's critical to success on the job. Carlo Maria Giulini, former conductor of the Los Angeles Philharmonic, once said about getting the job done that "what matters most is human contact." These traits should also be recorded in your Matching Qualifications Worksheet (Figure 3.1), in column B.

Elements to include in cover letter:

Introduction Opener (get attention by emphasizing perfect match)

Body Why you're applying (emphasize benefit to firm)
Your main qualifications (highlight a few)

Conclusion Request next step (interview or your phone call)

Figure 3.2

Outlining Your Cover Letter

A simple list of the items to include (Figure 3.2) works well as a preliminary outline and guide. In column C of your Matching Qualifications Worksheet, list the items from Figure 3.2, leaving four or five lines between them.

For each element, brainstorm ideas you might want to include. For example: your cover letter should include all of the format elements (although you needn't put them in the same exact order). Trying to force your ideas to fit a rigid format can end up sounding too stiff and formal. This will ultimately work against you. So the best advice is to use a natural style and keep it simple.

WRITING THE LETTER

Once you've completed your planning, you're ready to begin writing your draft letter. In case you haven't yet identified the specific job you're after, use sample ads to get ideas or simply conjecture the details of your ideal job. This first letter will be for practice. Once you know the job you're after you can tailor your letter accordingly. If you've done a good job outlining your ideas, all you need to do is follow your map to a winning cover letter. When you finish writing your practice cover letter, it's a good idea to put it aside for some time and then reread it for impact. It will sound new and fresh, as if you were reading it for the first time. You'll notice things you didn't see before, and you'll probably want to make a few changes to sharpen it up a bit. Another good way to get fresh ideas is to have a trusted colleague, friend, or family member read your cover letter before writing the final draft. File this draft in your Job Search Notebook until you're ready to send out your résumé. Then you can rewrite and tailor it to the particulars of each job.

From his well-constructed, detailed outline, it was easy for Brian to create a cover letter that was clear, concise, and direct. Because he did a careful analysis to match his qualifications to the job and then methodically outlined his opener, body, closing, and key points, he was able to make himself sound tailor-made for the position. At the same time, his letter (Figure 3.3) is objective and professional without the slightest hint of arrogance. Tim's letter (Figure 3.4), on the other hand, is an example of a poor letter portraying arrogance.

Opener

As the 18th-century English writer Samuel Johnson so aptly observed, "Confidence is the first requisite of achievement." Opening your cover letter with a self-assured attention grabber and closing with an assertive request will project the confidence you need for success. It's important to tailor both of these statements to your situation.

Confident openers are tricky. You want to get attention without running the risk of sounding gimmicky or arrogant. It's a fine line and requires some skillful handling. The letter in Figure 3.4 is a good example of someone who stepped over the line and fell into blatant arrogance. A staffing manager at a Fortune 500 consumer products

123 Willow Drive
Anywhere, USA 12345
January 9, 19__

Fortune 500 Company
456 Palm Drive
Los Angeles, CA 12345

Dear Sir/Madam:

tailored match

The Human Resource Specialist position you advertised in the *Sunday Times* immediately captured my attention as a perfect match for my qualifications. My background includes extensive experience in program design/delivery, group facilitation, needs analysis, and organization development in a corporate setting.

benefits

gets reader to look at résumé

Along with the benefits of my education and experience, I would bring exceptional human relations skill and a high level of energy and commitment to the job. I'd appreciate the opportunity to meet with you in person. You may reach me by phone at (123)456-7890. Thank you for considering me for a position with your firm.

Sincerely,

Brian Smith

Figure 3.3: Brian's Sample Cover Letter
Marginal notes indicate manager's comments.

firm shared this letter with me. Tim thought this would be an effective attention getter. Well, it did get him plenty of attention, but all of it was negative!

Rod took a different approach. He used an interesting unconventional attention getter, as you can see in Figure 3.5. The marketing recruiter who gave me this letter really liked the approach. I think it could work well in certain situations, although I think it very much depends on the industry. Creative, catchy approaches like this are often effective in marketing, advertising, art, or sales but would be considered frivolous in conservative businesses such as banking, insurance, or law. You need to decide based on the type of job you're applying for.

If you've met the employer or have been referred by a mutual acquaintance, you can use the opener to remind the reader of this.

When you have a personal relationship with the interviewer. Sam's letter applying for an internship to a professional association colleague opens with a crisp, confident statement:

> When we met at the Medical Society luncheon last week, you asked me to send you a résumé. While I'm happy with my present work, I'm naturally interested in new opportunities that promise more challenge and reward.

Sam's opener works well because it immediately identifies the business relationship and focuses on a confident interest in the opportunity. The approach is positive (no sour grapes about unhappiness).

I am 35 years old and in great health, 6'3" tall, blond, an all-American type with a million dollar (non-smoking) smile. My current compensation package exceeds $75,000.

I would be glad to discuss my experience and assets further in a personal interview.

Tim Thomas
123 Cedar Lane
Anywhere, USA 12345
Phone: (123)456-7890

Figure 3.4: Example of poor opener for cover letter
The hiring manager was very much turned off by this opener.

456 Oak Tree Rd.
Anywhere, USA 12345
June 10, 19—

[attach packet of instant coffee]

Fortune 500 Company
123 Sycamore Dr.
Los Angeles, CA 12345

Dear _____,

intro-duction The first cup is on me!

Take a break from your hectic day, get a cup of hot water, and make a cup of coffee. Sit back and take a moment to look over my résumé, and see if you agree that with 10 years of solid systems expe-

benefit rience and exceptional people skills, I have what you need to solve some of your programming/systems analysis problems.

why applying I am interested in relocating to the Southern California area in the near future, and I would like to obtain a position in which I can assist non-technical people in using complex computer systems.

next step Let's talk soon. I'll call you next week to arrange a candid interview. I'm sure we can work together to "brew up" a great team!

Sincerely,

Rod Johnson

Figure 3.5: Catchy Opener for Cover Letter
A gimmick like this can be a great attention-getter for employers in such fields as advertising, art, marketing, or sales—but a real mistake in others like banking, insurance, or law.

Sam shows a genuine interest in challenge and reward without sounding aggressive or arrogant.

A formal letter may be unnecessary if you've already talked with the manager. Often a personalized handwritten note is more effective when the employer is expecting your résumé.

When you have special experience. When you want to distinguish yourself by emphasizing your special experience or abilities, you can use an opener like Sharon's when she applied for an administrative assistant position.

> As assistant to the general manager of a major consumer research firm, I'm relied on heavily for my administrative and supervisory skills. A critical element is my exceptional interpersonal skill and ability to be tactful and discreet. I handle many confidential matters in dealing with executive management at the corporation.

This confident opener immediately distinguishes Sharon as a prime candidate. It's effective because it really adds valuable insight to the basic résumé information. This type of opener will also help recent grads gain points over other applicants by drawing attention to non-job experience which makes them uniquely qualified. For example, a junior accountant creatively highlighted the fact that she founded her college accounting society, and an assistant editor noted that she initiated a campus literary magazine. Additionally, the cover letter format allows you to add detail and enthusiasm for your profession which the résumé format does not.

Body of the Cover Letter

To construct the body of your letter, refer back to your Matching Qualifications Worksheet, column C. Here you should have recorded the details of why you're applying for the job (perfect match), your uniquely matched qualifications, and the benefit to the firm for hiring you. With this information already outlined, to construct the body of your letter, all you need to do is follow your map and create a sentence from each idea listed.

Close with Confidence

In closing, when you have the employer's phone number, you should offer to call the employer in about a week to set up an interview.

The guideline here is to take control whenever possible. It's always the person making the call who's in control. So, if you have the phone number, take control of the situation and make that call. If you don't have the number, request that the employer call you.

Compare Brian's letter to that of another applicant, Rachel (Figure 3.6) who applied for Brian's job. Because Brian took the time to find out more about the position, he was able to match his qualifications exactly to the job requirements. Rachel, on the other hand, blindly wrote her cover letter and, without doing any preliminary planning and research, she emphasized detailed university experience (Resource Ed.) that was important to her but irrelevant to the job. If she had done her research, Rachel would have learned that corporate experience was critical. With this knowledge, she could easily have

---

SUCCESS ENHANCER

Recent studies have found that up to 80 percent of one's success in business depends upon the ability to communicate effectively. Look around you. Who's getting promoted and moving ahead? In virtually every industry and at every level, it's the people who communicate well. They know how to persuade and to get their ideas across, both in writing and in person. You may have all the technical knowledge and skill of an Einstein, but it means nothing if you can't communicate.

How do you communicate well? First, pay attention—practice, practice, practice. Pick out someone who is a powerful communicator, and use that person as your communication role model. It could be a politician, a businessperson, a teacher, a boss, colleague, or even a friend or family member. Pay close attention to how that person communicates. What kind of vocabulary and sentence structure does he or she use? Does this person tell stories as analogies or use similes and metaphors to illustrate points? How does the person organize for persuasion?

You can improve your communication skills further by taking writing and public speaking classes, by reading up on the subject, or by listening to cassette tapes on communication techniques.

Try to write something every day (such as a letter or a journal), and get feedback on your writing from a reliable source so that you can correct your mistakes. Look for opportunities to volunteer for writing and speaking assignments. In addition to practice opportunities, these assignments will also give you visibility and help you build a reputation for energy and commitment.

Fortune 500 Company
456 Palm Drive
Los Angeles, CA 912345

Re: Training and Development Specialist

Dear Employer:

I have enclosed my résumé for your consideration for the above position.

detail not relevant to job at hand — Let me expand on my background that is pertinent to the position. I have presented programs for those who were just entering the world of commerce and production. I was part of a program that introduced a new manner of study at the University of Acme, School of Business, called Resource-Ed. (cassette and work book independent study). This enabled the student on a semester basis to acquire the same unit credit and subject grade as the student on campus. This delivery was solely for the undergraduate degree.

should add detail here related to job — In the years past I have prepared in-house training programs for many industries.

I would appreciate an appointment to further discuss the possibility of joining your organization.

Sincerely,

Rachel Brown

Figure 3.6: Rachel's Sample Cover Letter
Employer thought much of this detail was unrelated to the job requirements as stated in Figure 3.1.

downplayed the Resource Ed. and added valuable detail to the management, banking, and business training programs. Adding details such as presentation skill and group facilitation (which Brian learned were desired from his phone call to the employer) could have tailored Rachel's background to the position. Tailoring is the key to success in tough times.

Your Letter's Appearance

Attention to quality is absolutely paramount to your success! And to get the job you want, particularly in these competitive times, you must invest the necessary time and effort to produce meticulous quality in every aspect of your job search.

It is important to use professional looking stationery. Many make the mistake of thinking they must purchase expensive, colored bond for their cover letter. Not true. Plain white paper or inexpensive personalized stationery works just fine—as long as it's professional looking.

It should go without saying that carelessness in the appearance of a letter will definitely put it at the bottom of the pile (if not in the wastebasket). There's absolutely no excuse for it!

If you're unsure of your writing skills, grammar, punctuation, spelling, or typing skill, get help. Readily available aids include:

- typing/editing services
- librarians
- university hot lines
- courses
- seminars
- colleagues
- reference books
- consultants
- software

There are inexpensive software programs available at computer stores which will correct all spelling, grammar, punctuation, and capitalization errors. Additionally, many of these programs will make suggestions to sharpen vocabulary and improve sentence and paragraph structure. If you don't have access to a computer, try your local library. Many local libraries now rent computer time for word processing functions. It will be well worth your while to check out this opportunity and avoid the fatal mistakes Dina made.

If your typing skills are rusty or nonexistent (as Dina's were) it's well worth the investment to hire a typist. Many excellent typing/secretarial/editing services are available in every community. Check your local yellow pages, Chamber of Commerce, university, or college. Although typewriter print is acceptable, computer type is much more impressive these days. Check around and see what you can find that suits your budget. Remember, whatever you choose, it must be absolutely letter perfect, neat, and professional—just like your performance on the job. The checklist in Figure 3.8, "Cover Letter Do's and Don'ts," will help make your cover letter perfect.

I don't know where Dina and Tim are today. But I can assure you

---

XYZ Productions
Media Lane
Anywhere, USA 12345

incorrect punctuation

Dear Sirs:

typo — I'm interested in the assistant producers' position you advertised in the *Sunday Times*. My background es perfect for the job. I have Seven years experience working for a major studio. I assist with program design and handle all production detail.

should be lower case

In addition to my education (MA in Communication) I'm skilled in adminsitration and human relations.

misspelled word

I'll call you in about a week to set up a meeting.

address should be at top

Dina Harrison
123 Peach Tree Grove
Anywhere, USA 12345

Figure 3.7
Dina's background was a perfect match for the job she was applying for, but the manager refused to consider her because of her carelessness here.

that if they have new jobs, they "talked" their way into them without a cover letter. (More about verbal techniques in the chapters on interviewing.)

Over the years, managers from many different industries have

DO	DON'T
highlight special qualifications	mention being fired
quantify accomplishments	bad-mouth current employer
accentuate the positive	mention personal problems
emphasize what you bring to job	talk about personality conflicts
learn about firm and products	emphasize what the job will do for you
be self-confident	mention weaknesses
offer to contribute	go over 2–3 short paragraphs
emphasize mutual benefit	use flowery language
be creative	sound arrogant
get closure	use inappropriate gimmicks
tailor to industry and position	emphasize growth potential
say what you have to offer	sound rambling
state why you're interested	use run-ons or fragments
know when not to use cover letter	allow punctuation errors
remind of personal link	get too informal
use manager's name	close with "cordially" or "affectionately"
keep it short and professional	allow spelling errors
emphasize energy and commitment	allow typos
emphasize people skills	use dirty typewriter ribbon
use personalized stationery	make corrections in pen
use quality paper	put your address at the bottom of page
be neat and letter perfect	mention age
use correct typing format	mention personal details
get help proofreading and editing	
match qualifications to job	

Figure 3.8: Cover Letter Do's and Don'ts

shared their thoughts with me on these commonly asked questions regarding cover letters.

I've heard that the cover letter really doesn't matter because most managers don't read it. They go straight to the résumé. Is this true?

While this may be true in some instances, I think most managers do read the cover letter. It's an important part of your self-marketing strategy and it says a lot about you. What you may be referring to is a situation where the hiring manager already knows the applicant. In these cases, a cover letter is unnecessary.

How can I make myself seem perfect without sounding arrogant?

Remember, you're not trying to sound perfect—just perfect for the job at hand. You want to present yourself as a perfect fit for the job requirements. And the trick is to find out as much as you can about the job and then tailor your qualifications to match. This will make you seem perfect for the job.

How can I learn more about the job when I'm responding to a blind ad and there's no phone number to call?

A blind ad really does leave you pretty much in the dark on this. Since you won't be able to get the particulars on this specific job, you might try finding out about this type of job within the industry. Talk to people you've met through networking to see if they can give you insight into typically desirable qualities for this type of job. You can also research the industry at the library or college career center.

What is an appropriate salutation when you're not sure of the gender of the person you're addressing?

This is a controversial issue. Surveys of managers in various organizations have shown that the traditional, "Dear Sir" is still acceptable. However, as more women move up in the management ranks, sensitivity on this issue is increasing. Because of this sensitivity, I think you can reduce the risk of offending someone by using, "Ladies and Gentlemen" or "Dear Madam/Sir." A group of attorneys for whom I did a workshop once told me they prefer "Gentlepeople"! Of course, you should make every effort to get the name of the person you're addressing. When you have the phone number of the company, always call to get the hiring manager or representative's name and use it in the salutation.

What is the appropriate complimentary close for a cover letter?

A simple, "Sincerely" works best. "Very truly yours" would work, although this seems a bit formal. Definitely, you'll want to save "Cordially" and "Affectionately" for more personal letters. If you know the person you're writing to, "Sincerely" may seem a bit formal, in which case "Regards" works well.

Your cover letter is more than just an afterthought. It's a critical part of your self-marketing package because it introduces you, highlights your unique qualifications, makes you look perfect for the job, and gets your résumé read. Once you've followed the steps outlined in this chapter and written your winning cover letter, you're ready to write your résumé.

As you complete this chapter on writing the winning cover letter, you will have filed the following items in your **Job Search Notebook** under section three.

Matching Qualifications Worksheet

Draft Cover Letter

CHAPTER 4

The Well-Crafted Résumé: Tailoring Your Qualifications

"The difference between the right word and the almost-right word is the difference between lightning and the lightning bug."

—*Mark Twain*

I am often asked, "What's the purpose of the résumé, anyway? Is it to summarize my entire career? Is it to make myself look terrific? Is it to show that I'm the most qualified applicant?" My answer is "yes" to all of these. Now, you're probably thinking, "that's a tall order...where do I begin? How can I achieve all of this with one résumé?"

You need a focus, and that focus should be to tailor your qualifications to the job so that you get an interview. Getting the interview is of paramount importance because the interview gets you the job. Without the opportunity to interview, you're doomed to failure – and without a sharply tailored résumé to capture the employer's attention, you'll never get the interview. This chapter tells you how to put together a tailored résumé that's guaranteed to set you apart from the crowd. If you followed my advice in Chapter 3, you've already matched your qualifications to the job you want for a custom fit. You can now use this information to tailor you résumé accordingly, creating a résumé format for your particular situation.

THE BASIC CHRONOLOGICAL RÉSUMÉ AND HOW TO TAILOR IT

In putting together your tailored résumé, your first step should be to start thinking about the categories of information you'll want to include about yourself and your background. You can do this by establishing five pages in your Job Search Notebook (one for each of the categories). Then, file these pages in section 4 of your Job Search Notebook. I like to think of this process as creating a file for each category. We'll be discussing six basic categories here—not necessarily in the order they'll appear on your résumé. Appropriate order will be discussed later in the section on enhancing your background.

- career objectives
- education
- professional experience
- special skills
- achievements

These categories will help you to get started and keep your thoughts organized as you sort through your background to select the information tailored for the job you're after. Once you've outlined your ideas, created a basic chronological résumé, and have read the material in this chapter on enhancing your background, you can go back and modify these categories again to suit your special needs.

Career Objective

Your career objective tells what position you're after and where you want to go with your career. You should refer to the Career Goals section of your Job Search Notebook to review your ideas on this and help formulate your career objective.

Job seekers often wonder whether stating a career objective is really necessary. Experts disagree on this question. Many insist that without it your résumé is incomplete, while others advise everyone to forget it! My advice is to postpone your decision until you've done some analysis to determine whether a stated career objective will work for you. Before deciding to use a career objective, you should be sure that it will enhance your tailored approach and make you sound like a perfect fit for the job. Don't fall into the trap of sounding so general that your statement is absolutely meaningless as Maria, a junior accountant at a large chemical company, did when she wrote, "I'm seeking a position that will offer advancement and the opportunity to utilize my talent, education, and experience." Maria's mistakes here are focusing on what the job offers *her* (which sounds self-centered) and stating the obvious (since both employer and applicant know that the next step after junior accountant is accountant, then senior accountant). In Maria's case, the career objective is better left unsaid.

When is the career objective useful? It's important to declare your objectives in situations where they may be unclear to the reader—for instance when you're changing fields, seeking an entry level position, focusing a hopscotch pattern or clarifying multi-level options (director at small company or manager at large company). Often, the career objective can be discussed in your cover letter. This allows you to customize your objective for individual jobs without retyping your résumé. If you decide to use the career objective in your résumé, keep in mind that your statement of career objectives should be:

concise (1–2 sentences)

clear

specific and meaningful

job-focused (that is, not self-centered)

Following are sample career objectives from hiring managers in various fields that demonstrate a clear sense of purpose and career aspirations without sounding trite or self-centered. Each pertains to the job seeker's specific situation.

Changing Specializations: "My immediate goal is a position as a staff technician in a large teaching hospital. Through my work experience and part-time graduate study in laboratory procedures I plan to specialize in immunology. My ultimate goal is to instruct student technicians in this area."

Seeking Entry Level Position: "Entry-level staff accountant position."

Clarifying Multi-level Options: "Director of training and development for small company or senior staff position at large corporation."

Focusing a Hopscotch Pattern: "To work as pharmaceutical sales representative, continue my graduate studies in chemistry, and build on my sales/management experience, eventually assuming market management responsibilities."

Each job, each person, and each situation is unique; to be successful, you must tailor accordingly.

Education

If you're a recent grad with little or no work experience, your educational experience is the ticket and should be near the top of your résumé. However, if you have work experience, that experience becomes more important. Your work history and accomplishments should then be near the top of the résumé and your education near the bottom

Everything on your résumé should be focused to present your best image for a particular position. For this reason, you should list your education in reverse chronological order, putting your most advanced degree first. This helps to get attention and also to establish your credentials for the particular job. First, list your diploma if you have only high school (once you have a degree it's not necessary to list high school) or degree, and your major; next, list the name of the institution you attended, the city, and your year of graduation. List only the university from which you have actually graduated. Listing other schools you attended is not only unnecessary, but could also give an impression of instability.

You can also include options studied within your major. For example, Ted pursued a quality management option within an industrial technology major, which strengthened his qualifications for the job of manager of quality assurance. Other items that can strengthen your qualifications include special emphasis courses, educational internships, and research grants. (Internships may also be included under the professional experience category.)

SUCCESS ENHANCER

A good way to distinguish yourself is to develop a unique blend of specialties. One way to accomplish this is to take more classes in your chosen area of specialization. For example, a contract administrator who has also taken specialized courses in cost analysis and negotiation is much more valuable than a one-dimensional administrator.

Check the local chapter of your professional association or of a university extension for profession certifications in your field. Virtually every profession has certificate programs, which usually consist of five to ten college-level courses. Many professions also have qualifying exams that you can take to become licensed or certified in a particular area of expertise.

Right now, during your job search, is a good time to begin your courses. You can then add this to your résumé to enhance your professionalism.

Including professional certificates or specialized training in this section can be a real plus. It further qualifies you for a position and clearly demonstrates your commitment to professional growth and keeping current in your field. Linda, a junior designer for a small women's wear firm, knew the competition for the position of assistant department manager would be tough. Since she was the only applicant (both internally and externally) who had a professional certificate in business and management, in addition to the basic design degree, she scored critical points over her competition and got the job.

Impressive GPAs (3.0 and above) will work for you, especially if you're a recent grad. It's also a good idea to mention that you worked while going to school. (This should be included in the "Achievements" category of your résumé.) Many managers have told me that, from an employer's perspective, a graduate with a 3.4 who worked his or her way through school is more impressive than one with a 4.0 who didn't work. Once you have some work experience under your belt, the GPA becomes less important. A really impressive GPA (4.0) particularly in your major, will always work in your favor. As a hiring manager, I'm impressed with a 4.0!

As a recent grad or someone with limited experience in your field, you may want to highlight special areas of job-relevant training in which you've excelled. Listing six to eight courses with outstanding grades will work well for you. This strategy is particularly useful in highly specialized technical fields such as engineering, accounting, computer science, and law.

Class standing is another bit of information that can enhance your overall image. Anything in the top half is impressive. Rate yourself accordingly—top half, third, quarter, 10 percent and so on. Some schools include class standing on your grade transcript. It would be worthwhile to request an unofficial transcript and see what impressive data you can find. You might learn, for example, that although you had a lower overall GPA, your major and minor GPA was 4.0. This will look very good on your résumé, separating you from your competition.

Professional Experience

Experience is most often how the employer determines fit. Employers look at employment history and ask whether this candidate has the following attributes:

- the right kind of experience
- the right level of experience
- proven performance on the job
- the ability to learn
- the ability to fit in

Darlene Wilson
123 Peppertree Road
Anywhere, USA 12345
123-456-7890

clear, specific, job-focused objective

Career Objective: Computer Sales Representative

Education: B.S. 1991.
Major, Business Administration
Minor, Computer Science
Acme University, Anywhere, USA
GPA 3.8

a strong plus for recent grad

at beginning for recent grad

Professional Experience:

1988 to present
Sales Associate, Computertime Software, Anywhere, USA
- Handled software sales up to $100,000 per month
- Designed four successful sales promotions
- Promoted customer relations
- Managed inventory control
- Increased sales up to 50 percent per month

no need to mention part-time

quantifiables are strong

1986 to 1988
Commissioned Salesperson, ABC Department Store, Anywhere USA, Women's Clothing
- Handled Women's Clothing sales
- Promoted customer relations
- Highest sales in department every month
- Consistently ranked in top 10 percent of 100 regional salespersons

distinguishing factor

Professional Affiliations:
- National Retailers Association
- Student Computer Society

> Darlene Wilson
>
> **Special Skills:**
>
> - Hardware: Wang Office Information Systems and microcomputers, IBM AT, Zenith 248, other IBM-compatible microcomputers
> - Software: MS/DOS, Lotus 1-2-3, Lotus HAL, dBase III, WordPerfect, Wang Word Processing, Sidekick, Superproject Plus, Harvard Graphics, Microsoft Word
> - Exceptional persuasion and interpersonal skills
>
> **Achievements:**
>
> - Achieved 4.0 GPA in major and minor and 3.8 overall GPA
> - Earned 100 percent undergraduate expenses
> - Debate team champion for two consecutive years

specific knowledge applicable to job — (Special Skills)

shows good persuasive skills — (Achievements)

Figure 4.1
Sample chronological résumé format for recent grad with part-time work experience. Recent grads with no work experience should use functional résumé format, to be discussed later (Figure 4.7). Marginal notes represent hiring manager's comments.

This part of the résumé is your opportunity to provide all the right answers to these questions. You'll want to mold and shape your experience so that it's perfectly suited to your job. Of course, there are several formats to help you accomplish this: chronological, functional, combination, and technical. In the next section of this chapter we'll be discussing each of these in detail. For now, let's concentrate on the chronological as a basic format. Figures 4.1 and 4.2 provide samples of chronological résumés: one for someone with years of full-time work experience, one for a recent grad with only part-time work experience. These examples give a good overview of all categories

Paul West
123 Lemon Tree Lane
Anywhere, USA 12345
123-456-7890

clear & specific

Career Objective: Senior System Administrator

Professional Experience:
1986–Present   Davis Corporation, Anywhere, USA

Wang System Administrator—Oversee the daily operations of a Wang VS-100 system consisting of over 150 peripherals.
- Troubleshoot hardware/software/application problems
- Establish and maintain the security system

quantify when possible

- Train users (100–150)
- Write unique glossaries (macros)
- Write and maintain operating procedures and user reference manuals
- Interact with service technicians

1980–1986   ABC International Corporation, Anywhere USA

Word Processor-Specialist—Used a Multimate System for creating, revising, and editing various documents. These included: internal/external correspondence, proposals, statistical tables, charts, and various reports requiring the knowledge and use of special technical skills.

Working knowledge of
- MS/DOS
- Multimate
- MacDraw
- Microsoft Word
- Word Perfect

> Paul West
>
> **Achievements:**
> - Served as editor of civic organization newsletters
> - Won Publisher's Award for best civic organization newsletter in the state
> - Designed and instructed Office Systems course (beginners and advanced) for over 100 corporate employees
>
> **Education:**
> ACE High School, Diploma 1980
> Anywhere, USA

shows commitment (margin note beside Achievements)

at end for experienced worker (margin note beside Education)

Figure 4.2
Sample Chronological Résumé format for someone with solid work experience. Marginal notes highlight what reviewers like.

discussed. Once you've developed your chronological résumé based on these samples, you will file your draft in section 4 of your Job Search Notebook.

Even if you decide that one of the other résumé formats will best highlight your strengths, I recommend that you first outline your employment history chronologically. This exercise will provide several benefits for you. It will help you to identify patterns and skill clusters that can later be reformatted to your advantage, and it can help you see how certain jobs could appear undesirable or unrelated to your overall goals. (During the revision process, these can be de-emphasized with the right format.)

After centering your address and phone number at the top of the page, begin your chronology by listing the dates of each job, with the most recent at the top (see Figure 4.2). Next to the date, put the name and location of each employer. Under this, you should list your job title. If you feel that your job title isn't very descriptive of your position, you'll score points for clarifying with descriptive detail. But you should *never lie*: this will get you in trouble every time! Even if your cover is successful for awhile, it will ultimately work against you. I was once applying for a job in training, and I thought it would be useful to change the title of my current job—from "coordinator" to "training coordinator," because training was a large part of what I did. This clarification worked well in focusing my experience for my new job. However, it would have been a mistake for me to change my title to "training manager." That kind of misrepresentation would have quickly discredited me.

Next, under each job title, include a dynamic description of your responsibilities. It's important to remember that your reader has neither the time nor the inclination to sift through tedious detail. Simplicity is paramount. Four or five short sentences should be the maximum length for each description. Starting each sentence with a dynamic verb will grab your reader's attention and present you as an action-oriented achiever. Words like "initiated," "developed," "designed," and "directed" give an authoritative ring of achievement to your résumé. Using a dash or "bullet" before each sentence makes for easier reading because it breaks up the solid prose that can make reading seem more tedious. The list of dynamic verbs in Figure 4.3 will give you some ideas for strengthening your descriptions.

In addition to being concise and dynamic, another key to effective descriptions is focus. Your prospective boss doesn't need to know the nitty-gritty of your duties. Rather, he or she will want to know how your responsibilities fit into your organization. Focus on your contributions to the department and company goals. Rather than emphasizing duties, highlight results and achievements. Instead of just saying that he was responsible for work flow systems, Barry, a production specialist for a small division of a processed foods conglomerate, showcased the fact that he had designed a department workflow system that had resulted in an annual cost savings to the company of $18,000.

Being specific will force you to focus on results. Quantify everything. For example:

How many people report to you?

What is the dollar amount of your budget?

What is the dollar value of your department tasks (sales, contracts, procurements, etc.)?

How many pages were in the publication you produced/edited?

How many courses did you design and teach?

By what percent did you increase sales/profits/enrollments and so on?

By what percent did you reduce backlog, complaints, or rework?

How long did it take you solve a particular major problem?

Dynamic Verbs for Résumés

achieved	established	originated
added	evaluated	oversaw
addressed	executed	performed
administered	expanded	pioneered
analyzed	expedited	planned
arranged	experienced	prepared
assembled	facilitated	presented
assessed	formed	procured
assisted	formulated	produced
appeared	founded	promoted
automated	gained	provided
built	generated	recommended
clarified	handled	reduced
conceived	identified	reorganized
conducted	implemented	researched
constructed	improved	resolved
consulted	increased	selected
contributed	initiated	served
controlled	innovated	simplified
converted	inspired	simulated
coordinated	installed	sold
correlated	integrated	solved
counseled	interviewed	structured
created	introduced	succeeded
delegated	invented	supervised
demonstrated	justified	synchronized
designed	keynoted	synthesized
detailed	launched	systematized
developed	lectured	tailored
devised	maintained	taught
directed	managed	trained
discovered	marketed	transformed
doubled	motivated	united
earned	negotiated	verified
edited	operated	won
engineered	organized	wrote

Figure 4.3

Start each sentence of your responsibility description with a dynamic verb to portray yourself as an action-oriented achiever.

Being specific about how you fit into your organization is another good way to highlight your stature.

Who do you report to?

Do you report to your boss's boss in his or her absence?

Do you work on corporate-wide projects?

Do you work with executive management on special assignments?

Which functions report to you?

How many new products did you launch?

If you won an award or broke performance records, listing these will reinforce your achievement image. Dave managed the most profitable unit in his district, a medium-size hospital supply company. This is an impressive accomplishment that can set him apart from the competition. But awards don't have to be the high visibility type to impress. Many departments award internal recognition for small contributions which can look quite impressive on your résumé. For example, Sue, an insurance claims adjustor at a major firm, once received a suggestion award for recommending that housekeeping place saucers under plants in the lobby to prevent water leakage. For this she received a certificate which said "…for your outstanding contribution to productivity"! So she updated her résumé to read, "Won award for outstanding contribution to productivity." The point here is to creatively use what you have to demonstrate achievement and commitment. In these tough times, employers aren't looking for a nine-to-fiver who merely performs duties. They're looking for someone who does what it takes to get results—someone with a high performance track record, and that's precisely what you want to project in your employment history.

Professional Affiliations

Listing professional affiliations can strengthen your image of professionalism and commitment.

If you're a recent grad or a job seeker with limited experience, you can effectively use professional affiliations to enhance your professional image. Details of this strategy were discussed earlier in Chapter 1.

To be effective, your list of professional affiliations needs to be tailored to the position you're seeking. List no more than three or four affiliations and make sure they're relevant to your job. Listing too many or ones that aren't related can work against you and make you seem unfocused.

It's also a good idea to avoid listing organizations that could reveal a bias. Sexism and other biases are an unfortunate reality in business. For example, involvement in several women's organizations could lead the employer to think that you're an activist. Marilyn, a manager at a small advertising agency, fell into this trap by listing several professional associations for women, thinking this would demonstrate an interest in community service and professional dedication. However, an employment counselor pointed out that it made her sound like a female activist, an image that in many situations would work against her.

Be careful to select professional associations that are widely recognized in your industry. It's worthwhile to do some research and identify the most powerful associations. This may seem like a minor issue but it can help score important points with employers. I've seen managers make hiring decisions based on this. When the chips are down and all else is equal between two candidates, the one with the best connections has the advantage.

Although you'll want to list any offices held or special contributions to the association, it's a good idea to limit this kind of information. Many employers are concerned about overcommitment in this area. They don't want to hire someone who will give priority to association duties at the risk of being distracted from his own work.

If you aren't currently associated with any professional organizations, this is something you might want to consider doing as a way of getting more involved and adding a touch of professionalism to your résumé. Every industry and every community has many worthwhile organizations that could work well for you. If you need help locating one, try asking experienced professionals in your field who you've met through networking. College instructors, career counselors, and local librarians can also be very helpful.

Special Skills

This is a pivotal area of the résumé but one that is often overlooked by job seekers. In this area, you can showcase your unique talents, telling your prospective employer what you have to offer over and above job requirements that sets you apart from your competitors. Often employers are looking for a special blend of talent to fill a particular niche. For instance, a small graphics firm was looking for an art director, and they were delighted to find one who could also do special editing projects. The artist, Chuck, listed editing as a special skill, and this gave him an edge over the competition. This edge won the job!

Special skills most often appreciated in business (and not always mentioned in ads) are:

>being able to speak a second language

>knowledge of selected computer programs

>ability to operate special equipment

>ability in writing, editing, and public speaking

>teaching and presentation skills

>special industry-specific skills

>unique skill combinations (such as Chuck's)

The upcoming section on creative ways to enhance your experience gives more specific tips on how to use special skills to your advantage.

Achievements

Here is where you add everything you've done that can make you outstanding. You can even repeat some items that you've already mentioned in other areas. After all, in selling yourself, a little repetition for emphasis can be very effective. Be creative in this section. Let your professional image shine through. Whether you're a recent grad or experienced professional, the achievements section provides an excellent opportunity to highlight your strengths. Some items to include are:

>awards

>honors

>dean's list

>high GPA (over 3.0)

>high placement in graduating class (top 50 percent)

>scholarships

>publications

>listing in *Who's Who* and other publications

>radio and T.V. appearance

>offices held

percentage of college expenses earned

speeches made

internships

fellowships

new products launched

For easy reading, achievements should be listed one per line with a bullet or a dash before each line. This is an excellent way to conclude your résumé because you're leaving the reader with a strong positive image of yourself as a high achiever.

Figure 4.4 shows Mark's résumé for a consumer products marketing manager/director position in a hard-to-follow format that does not highlight his strengths to full advantage.

The revised version of Mark's résumé (Figure 4.5) following my suggested chronological format highlights his strengths to the maximum.

ENHANCING YOUR BACKGROUND

Building the right experience base can be a real dilemma for many job seekers. The old Catch 22 still applies: You need experience to qualify for the job; but if you don't get the job, how will you ever get the experience you need? This dilemma can plague almost any job seeker, and particularly those seeking new challenges (for example, people reentering the work force, recent grads, career changers, those with diverse experience, and those who have been in one job for a long time).

What if:

you don't have any specific qualifications?

your experience is outdated?

your qualifications are weak?

your experience is narrow?

you've had only one long-term specific job with a single employer?

your experience isn't in the right field?

The key is to build on what you have. You'll need to take inventory of what you've already accomplished and ask yourself, "How can I creatively present this in a way that will qualify me for the job I want?"

Mark Johnson
123 Lotus Lane
Anywhere, USA 12345
123-456-7890

needs objective

SUMMARY OF QUALIFICATIONS:

not focused: too many different areas

- Nine years experience in all phases of administration
- Five years experience in the development and implementation of marketing projects and programs
- Excellent organizational, time management, and communication skills
- Knowledge of Microsoft Word, Lotus 1-2-3, Quattro, and WordPerfect
- One year purchasing experience
- Familiarity with blueprint reading
- Four years consumer products experience

EDUCATION:

should be at end

B.S. Business Administration/Marketing,
Acme University, Anywhere, USA
M.S. Marketing,
Acme University, Anywhere, USA

EXPERIENCE:

MARKETING DIRECTOR
General Products Co. 3/88–11/90

unbroken narrative is hard to read

Orchestrated all phases of new packaging development as well as changes to existing packaging. Developed and maintained competitive profiles. Performed pricing analysis and comparisons to industry competitors' product pricing.

NEW PRODUCTS MANAGER
Consumer Products 2/86–12/88

dates are buried in narrative

Established purchasing sources and specifications for all components of a new products on

Mark Johnson

the bill of materials. Managed product flow from inception to rollout. Responsible for creation of promotional materials such as header cards, point of purchase displays, catalog sheets, and ad slicks.

MARKETING PROMOTIONS COORDINATOR
Retailer Products
Coordinated introduction of new products, co-op advertising, in-store promotions, and product testing. Compiled bimonthly sales alerts, monthly newsletters, and maintained communications with national sales force. Created product packaging and advertising through the use of PageMaker, graphic design, and camera techniques.

MANAGER
Consumer Plus, Inc. 2/84–2/86
Managed Los Angeles field office including responsibility for staff of 25. Maintained all internal accounting procedures including job costing, billing, payroll, and purchasing. Position required extensive client interface, including coordinating market research projects, focus groups, and field operations.

Figure 4.4: Example of poorly formatted résumé Special skills, achievements and professional affiliations are left out. Narrative format does not highlight accomplishments. Dates are hard to follow. Personnel specialists frown on this.

Mark Johnson
123 Lotus Lane
Anywhere, USA 12345
123-456-7890

clear multilevel objective

Career Objective:

Marketing director with small company or marketing manager with large to medium size company

Professional Experience:

easy to follow dates

3/88–11/90 **Marketing Director, General Products, Co., Anywhere, USA**

bullet format highlights accomplishments

- Orchestrated all phases of new packaging development as well as changes to existing packages
- Developed and maintained competitive profiles
- Performed pricing analysis and comparisons to industry competitors' product pricing
- Increased sales by 50 percent for two consecutive years

2/87–2/88 **New Products Manager, Retailer Products, Anywhere, USA**

dynamic qualifications

- Established purchasing sources and specifications for all components of a new product
- Managed product flow from inception to rollout for 25 diverse products
- Created promotional materials such as header cards, point of purchase displays, catalog sheets, and ad slicks

quantifiables add credibility

- Improved product flow time by 15 percent on 3 major products

Mark Johnson

2/87–2/88 Marketing Promotions Coordinator, Retailer Products, Anywhere, USA

- Introduced new products, co-op advertising, in-store promotions, and product testing
- Designed bimonthly sales alerts and monthly newsletters
- Initiated a communications network with national sales force
- Created product packaging and advertising through the use of graphic design and camera techniques
- Promoted to New Products Manager

listing promotions a plus

9/84–2/86 Manager, Consumer Plus, Inc., Los Angeles

- Managed Los Angeles field office including responsibility for staff of 25
- Managed all internal accounting procedures including job costing, billing, payroll and purchasing
- Handled extensive client interface, including coordinating market research projects, focus groups, and field operations
- Increased number of accounts by 25 percent representing over $1MM in annual sales

Professional/Community Affiliations:

- National Marketing Association, Speakers Bureau
- Central City Chamber of Commerce

Mark Johnson

use identification on each page in case it becomes detached

Special Skills:

- Blueprint reading
- Page Maker, Lotus 1-2-3, Word Perfect
- Graphic design
- Camera techniques
- Exceptional organization and productivity
- Communication and human relations

Achievements:

- Won ABC graduate fellowship
- Earned 100 percent expenses through undergraduate and graduate school
- Served as editor of college newspaper
- Addressed over 20 professional groups for National Marketing Association
- Completed requirements for Certified Marketing Managers exam. Will take exam 6/92.

Education:

- M.S., Marketing,
  Acme University, Anywhere, USA, 1984
- B.S., Marketing,
  Acme University, Anywhere, USA, 1982
  4.0 GPA in major

Figure 4.5
After revision, Mark's résumé portrays an accomplished achiever who is full of energy and commitment to his profession. Impressive to any employer!

Studies have shown that most people today change jobs several times before they reach 30. It's smart to experiment and try out different roles and companies before deciding what's right for you. This popular career strategy has several advantages:

helps you move up faster

provides broader experience

exposes you to different work climates

allows you to deal with diverse management styles

Job hopping, however, can create some disadvantages in a career plan, particularly when you're putting together a résumé for yet another new job. How do you make sense out of your patchwork quilt experience base? The functional résumé or combination résumé will help you focus.

As an established professional with solid experience in a single field, you may be involved in a job search for various reasons:

relocation with spouse

layoffs in your industry

dissatisfaction with current employer

Whatever the reason for your search, your goal will be the same—challenge and upward mobility. The task of putting together a résumé can seem overwhelming for someone who's been working steadily at the same job or at the same company for a number of years. Your main challenge will be to enhance your one-dimensional experience to qualify for your target job. The technical or combination format will help you highlight growth.

Figure 4.6 outlines three creative résumé formats:

functional – emphasizes skills

technical – focuses on specialization

combination – combines different types

The right format for you depends on your situation. The right one will showcase your talents, skills, and experience, while de-emphasizing anything in your background that's not right for the job you're after. Figures 4.7, 4.8, and 4.9 show good examples of functional, technical, and combination résumés.

Enhancing Limited Experience: The Functional Résumé

With its emphasis on skills, the functional résumé allows you to highlight what you can do for an employer. This is critical in tough

Type	Definition	Best For	Advantages
Chronological (Basic)	Lists employment history in reverse chronological order.	Those with lots of promotions and steady employment.	Easy to read Easy to prepare Most widely used Highlights steady employment
Functional	Lists skills learned on the job or through volunteer work. Organized into categories that relate to new job requirements.	Recent grads and those re-entering the work force. Those with limited experience or one long-time job. Job hoppers who need to focus experience. Career changers.	Focused and concise Spotlights most relevant areas Conceals employment gaps Conceals lengthy plateau
Technical	Lists areas of specialization, special emphasis courses, and special projects in addition to basic résumé components.	Those in technical fields such as engineering, math, science, computers, accounting. Those with limited experience. Recent grads.	Highlights special training Provides specifics on course and projects
Combination	Outlines chronology of work history and lists skills demonstrated on each job.	Works well for most people, particularly those with only one job and those changing career.	Highlights skills Shows steady employment

Figure 4.6: Creative Résumé Types

Thomas White
123 Lemon Lane
Anywhere, USA 12345

clear, concise objective

CAREER OBJECTIVE: Restaurant Manager

degree is an important plus so it goes up front

EDUCATION: B.S. Business Administration, 1991, Acme University, Anywhere, USA

SKILLS SUMMARY:

Management:

skill areas focus hopscotch job pattern

- Supervised ten employees
- Developed productive relationship with management, peers, and customers
- Promoted sales through effective planning, ordering, and advertising

Problem Solving:

- Designed communication system to expedite material from suppliers to restaurant
- Improved work flow systems which increased service efficiency and sales by 40 percent per quarter

quantifiables are impressive

Numerical Skills:

- Corrected and prevented $2,000 annual losses
- Revamped annual budgeting process, cutting preparation time in half with new software

Public Relations:

- Responsible for directing and coordinating publicity activities
- Communicate with wide range of customers and suppliers

Thomas White

Professional Experience:

9 years of hopscotch pattern need little detail

- Waiter, XYZ Restaurant (1 year)
- Assistant Manager, Fine Food Restaurant (2 years)
- Manager, Fine Food Restaurant (3 years)
- Sales Associate, Ace Real Estate (3 years)

Professional Affiliations:

shows commitment

- National Restauraters Association
- National Sales Association

Achievements:

- Worked 40+ hours per week as restaurant assistant manager and manager while attending college part-time
- Achieved 3.5 GPA in major

Figure 4.7
Sample Functional Résumé format for someone with experience (worked full-time while earning degree) Marginal notes represent personnel director's comments.

times. It plays up what you have to offer and downplays experience weaknesses. The key to creating an effective functional résumé is being able to ferret out your skills. I've often counseled recent grads and women reentering the job market who think they don't have any skills. My job search clients, Ryan and Claudia, are good examples. Neither had ever held a paid job. After we talked and I learned more about their backgrounds, it became clear that they had a wealth of experience and a lot to offer a prospective employer. To identify your own skills, write down everything you've done in the areas that follow. Listing these items will help you ferret out some of your hidden skills.

Nicole Nicholas
123 Raspberry Lane
Anywhere, USA 12345
123-456-7890

clear, specific objective

Career Objective:
Entry Level Government Revenue Officer

degree & GPA are important for recent grad

Education: B.A. Accounting, 1992
Acme University, Anywhere, USA (3.5 GPA)

Special Emphasis Courses:

special courses show depth & expertise

- Auditing Principles
- Advanced Accounting
- Cost Accounting
- General Accounting
- Managerial Accounting
- Principles of Accounting
- Income Tax I & II
- Business Statistics I & II

demonstrates ability

School Projects:
Served as Vice-President of Finance for mock corporation with $1 Billion annual sales. Won Most Profitable Enterprise Award (Business Management Class).

Special Skills:
- Lotus 1-2-3
- MS/DOS
- Microsoft Word

Work Experience:
1985 – Present
Bookkeeper, XYZ Company, Anywhere, USA
- Managed Accounts Payable, Receivable, and Payroll
- Trained and supervised Assistant Bookkeeper

> Nicole Nicholas
>
> **Professional Affiliations:**
> - Accountants International
>
> **Achievements:**
> - Worked 10 hours a week as bookkeeper while attending school full-time
> - Earned 4.0 GPA in major
> - Won ABC state scholarship
>
> 2 of 2

Figure 4.8
Sample Technical Résumé Format for a recent grad with limited work experience. Marginal notes represent staffing representative's comments.

School Organizations (student government, speech/drama club, newspaper, sports, fraternity/sorority, service organization, photography club)

Civic Organizations (Junior Achievement, Rotary, Kiwanis, Lions, community theater)

Charitable Organizations (Heart Association, March of Dimes, hotlines, clothing drives, fund-raisers, library association, scholarship group)

Church Activities and Organizations (fund-raisers, committees, programs, Sunday school)

Offices Held (committee chair, club president)

Special Projects (What were they and what results were achieved?)

Professional Services—for family and friends (accounting major doing taxes, law major giving advice, business major balancing budget, etc.). This can be identified as special skills and listed as freelance experience.

Figures 4.10 and 4.11 outline ideas for converting volunteer experience to specific job qualifications. Complete and file your list of these items and Figures 4.10 and 4.11 in your Job Search Notebook under section 4.

Once you've identified your job-related skills and experience, you're ready to begin creating your résumé. If you've followed my

Sandra Samuels
123 Oakridge Lane
Anywhere, USA 12345
123-456-7890

Experience Summary:
highlighting years of experience downplays absence
- 8 years comprehensive experience printing
- 10 years experience in graphic design
- 8 years management and supervisory experience

Career Objective: Art/Graphics Manager

Education: B.A. Fine Arts (1985), ACME University, Anywhere, USA

Professional Experience:

1986–1991 **General Manager, Family Business, Anywhere, USA**

home management experience builds skill
- Responsible for productivity, quality, strategic planning, balancing the budget, team building, and staff development

1980–1986 **Graphics Manager, Gordon's Publishing, Anywhere, USA**
- Changed company sales emphasis to large volume accounts
- Developed and maintained extensive filing system of critical job materials and data
- Instituted expediting procedures
- Held regular conferences with clients on job status
- Supervised employees to insure that all jobs were completed to each client's specifications

Sandra Samuels

1981–1986 Assistant Manager
all jobs including:
- Consulted with clients to formulate job concept
- Created and produced creative graphic design
- Estimated job costs
- Organized layout and paste-up of monthly publications
- Prepared layouts and paste-up on booklets, pamphlets, posters, flyers, brochures, catalog sheets, letterheads, envelopes, business cards, forms

Special Skills:
Extensive knowledge in operation of:
- Addressograph
- IBM Composer (non-justified copy)
- Kenro Vertical 18 inch Camera
- Pako Processor
- Robertson Photo Mechanix Horizontal Camera

Professional Affiliations:
- National Graphics Association
- Artists International

Achievements:
- Earned 100 percent of undergraduate expenses
- Worked 40 hours per week while attending college
- Achieved 4.0 in major
- Served as layout manager of civic organization newsletter (1986–1991)

Figure 4.9
Sample Combination Résumé format for someone reentering the workforce after five year absence. Marginal notes represent hiring manager's comments.

VOLUNTEER EXPERIENCE—CLAUDIA	JOB QUALIFICATIONS
Church Fundraiser-Chairperson *Skills Area* Finance, Business Management	

Volunteer skills:
- organization
- leadership
- management
- marketing
- advertising
- creativity
- communication
- computers/software
- motivation
- planning

Job qualifications:
- public speaking
- conducting meetings
- coordinating
- group dynamics
- bookkeeping
- problem solving
- decision making
- public relations
- goal setting
- tax reports

Civic Organization Newsletter
Skills Area
Communication, Publications

Volunteer skills:
- supervision
- human relations
- interpersonal skills
- art/graphics
- communication
- computers/software
- design/layout
- editing
- writing
- interviewing

Job qualifications:
- recruiting
- motivating
- chairing meetings
- coordinating
- planning
- managing diverse groups
- feedback
- problem solving
- decision making

Child Care Co-op Manager
Skills Area
Management, Administration

Volunteer skills:
- organization
- leadership
- management
- supervision
- human relations
- interpersonal skills

Job qualifications:
- communication
- budget management
- computers/software
- administration
- assessment
- public speaking

> - chairing meetings
> - coordinating
> - group dynamics
> - managing diverse groups
> - evaluation
> - feedback
>
> - coaching
> - public relations
> - conflict resolution
> - problem solving
> - decision making
>
> 2 of 2

Figure 4.10
Try to identify at least three experiences from home, school, church, civic or charitable organizations. Focus on skill areas and brainstorm to find possible job qualifications, as Claudia did.

suggestions at the beginning of this chapter, you already have your basic information outlined in a chronological format. You have a good start and a solid foundation. Your task now is to revise and enhance. The functional format allows you to showcase your buried talents. You'll file the draft of your tailored résumé in section 4 of your Job Search Notebook.

You've already carefully worded your first two résumé components, career objective, and education in the beginning of this chapter when you outlined your chronological résumé. These will remain the same. In the functional résumé, instead of putting professional experience next, you're going to create a new section called **Skills Summary**. In this section, you'll organize your job-related skills (which you identified in Figures 4.10 and 4.11) into categories which apply directly to the job at hand.

Claudia was a recent college grad with a degree in business administration seeking a management trainee position. She was convinced that as a housewife who took ten years to get her degree, she didn't have any worthwhile experience until she did the skills listing and qualifications conversion (Figures 4.10 and 4.11). She was amazed at the number of marketable skills she'd accumulated with just a few years of very spotty volunteer work.

I asked Claudia to explore the job-related skills developed through her studies and at home. As a business administration major, she'd gained several valuable skills that she previously hadn't considered. It doesn't matter what your major is, if you've successfully completed college-level courses, you've gained transferable skills. And you need to showcase these skills for your prospective employer. Housewives also develop many marketable skills through their home management experience.

Your next step is to create three or four career-related categories that fit your job such as management, finance, communication, or public relations. Then you can begin to list your specific skills and experiences under each category. The most effective format for this is to use four or five one-line descriptors. This format will highlight about twenty solid skills and experiences qualifying you for the job you're seeking. (See Figure 4.12 for example.)

If you have any work experience at all (part-time, summer job, volunteer work, or even work unrelated to career goals), you can list it here. You're probably wondering how you can possibly make these experiences sound relevant. The key is the flexible format. (See Figure 4.12.) Unlike the chronological format, you don't need to fully describe each position and give dates. You may want to list only company names. You'll give dates and position titles only when it's to your advantage. You may want to avoid names, titles, and dates altogether, simply stating in general terms something like, "earned 100 percent expenses through high school and college" or "worked full-time during summers and part-time during school since 19__ at such jobs as waitress, cashier, teaching assistant, and library aide."

Home Management

- flexibility
- multiple priorities
- balancing budget
- prioritization
- team building
- organization
- creativity
- conflict resolution
- interpersonal skills
- planning
- problem solving
- motivating a staff
- delegation
- follow-through
- strategic planning
- staff development

School

- organizing ideas
- critical reading
- time management
- prioritization
- following instructions
- problem solving
- analytical thought
- planning
- team projects
- presentation skills
- meeting deadlines
- follow-through
- evaluation
- assessment techniques
- creativity
- goal setting

Figure 4.11
Claudia's Job-Relevant Skills Learned at Home and in School

Claudia Jones
123 Willow Grove
Anywhere, USA 12345
123-456-7890

clear, specific career goal

CAREER OBJECTIVE: Entry level manager trainee in retail banking.

degree is important for recent grad

EDUCATION: B.S. Business Administration Acme University, Anywhere, USA, 1990.

SKILLS SUMMARY:

works well for someone with no paid work experience

Management
- Supervision. Managed staff of 15 at co-op school of 150 students. Developed successful relationships with staff, parents, children.
- Training. Developed and implemented ten-hour new staff and in-service training programs.
- Public Relations. Controlled communication with sponsors and community.
- Conflict Resolution. Resolved disagreements between staff and customers.
- Meeting Leadership. Planned and conducted monthly staff meetings and quarterly development meetings.

Finance
- Budget Management. Controlled budgets for co-op school and church development committee.
- Tax Reports. Prepared annual tax returns for six clients. Managed balance sheets for $1MM two-year development program.

Claudia Jones

quantify when possible

- Business Management. Revamped annual budgeting process, cutting preparation time in half with new software.
- Bookkeeping. Designed new system for speed and accuracy with figures. Worked efficiently with money. Corrected and prevented $2,000 annual losses.

Communication
- Publications. Directed and coordinated publicity activities for 150-member organization.
- Writing. Exceptional writing skill. Edited and produced monthly five-page newsletter for three years.
- Interpersonal Skills. Demonstrated exceptional skill in communicating with wide range of clients. Won their confidence and cooperation.

WORK EXPERIENCE:
- Manager, ABC Child Care Co-op (5 years)
- Editor, YWCA Newsletter (3 years)
- Vice-President, Church Development (2 years)
- Consultant, freelance tax preparation and balance sheets (3 years)

PROFESSIONAL AFFILIATIONS:
- USA Banker's Association, Speakers Bureau
- Toastmasters International

Claudia Jones

SPECIAL SKILLS:
- Graphics/layout
- Writing/editing
- MS/DOS
- Lotus 1-2-3
- Word Perfect
- analytical thought
- problem solving
- goal setting
- follow-through
- prioritization

ACHIEVEMENTS:

will help distinguish you from other entry-level applicants

- Worked 20 hours per week as Manager of child care co-op while attending college full-time.
- Served as Editor of civic organization newsletter. Won Publisher's award for best newsletter in the state.
- Completed two courses toward Certified Banking Managers exam. Will take exam 6/92.
- Achieved 4.0 GPA in major.
- Served as Financial Vice-President of Student Business Association.

3 of 3

Figure 4.12
Sample Functional Résumé for someone with no paid work experience. Marginal notes represent manager's comments

When you've completed the work experience section, go back to the basic chronological résumé you prepared in the first part of this chapter and pick up your final sections on:

professional affiliations

special skills

achievements

The functional format offers many advantages. It's flexible and creative. It allows a job seeker to identify and highlight assets and talents relevant to a particular job. It clearly demonstrates that valuable points toward job qualifications can be scored in arenas other than work history. This is important in a difficult job market. It will help you make the most of everything you have and put your best foot forward.

Highlighting Special Skills: The Technical Résumé

Using a special format designed for technical fields allows an applicant to highlight specific, detailed information which is important to many employers in technical areas such as:

engineering

science

computers

mathematics (statistician)

medicine

law

accounting

In addition to your basic résumé components, the technical format:

identifies areas of specialization

lists special emphasis courses and grades

highlights special training

provides specifics on projects

includes overall GPA

includes GPA in major

If you followed my suggestions earlier in this chapter, you've already prepared your carefully worded sections on Career Objective and Education. In preparing your technical résumé, you can now pick up those two items and use them near the top of your résumé. After you list your degree, you should include your overall GPA and GPA in your major field. (see Figure 4. 13).

Then list any special emphasis courses which you feel will be an advantage in the job you're after. This list can include up to a dozen or so courses. You should also include your grade for each course. Usually, A's and B's will work for you. It's probably better to leave off any courses where you earned lower than a B.

Next list two to five special projects related to your career goal. This will identify you as a specialist in these areas which could be the

Ryan Browning
123 Apple Orchard Rd.
Anywhere, USA 12345
123-456-7890

CAREER OBJECTIVE:

clear, concise objective

Programmer/Systems Analyst

EDUCATION: B.S. Computer Science, Acme University, Anywhere, USA 1989 (4.0 GPA)
M.B.A., University of Acme, Anywhere, USA to be conferred April 1991 (3.8 GPA)

SPECIAL EMPHASIS COURSES:
- Engineering Probability and Statistics
- Numerical Analysis
- Digital Computer Architecture
- Logic Design
- Automata and Formal Languages

SCHOOL PROJECTS:

demonstrate area of expertise

- Developed word processor in Ada, using packages, generics, exception handling, and separate compilation.
- Developed program in C, using monitors, message passing, and synchronization process, to ensure mutual exclusion for parallel processes on the UNIX operating system.
- Designed spelling check program in LISP and PROLOG.

SPECIAL SKILLS:
- FORTRAN
- PASCAL
- Lotus
- Graphwriter
- IBM DOS 3.3
- BASIC
- FOCUS
- dBase III
- Harvard Graphics
- Microsoft Word

Ryan Browning

- UNIX
- Excel
- Word Perfect
- Teaching all levels of computer skills
- Exceptional organizational/planning ability

WORK EXPERIENCE:
ABC Division of Softek International Corporation
Programmer Analyst/Software Instructor

1990–present
- (20 hours per week) Junior Analyst

1987–1990
- Conducted classroom computer training for 500 engineers, and individualized consulting
- Provided microcomputer technical support for the $1BB ASB project

1986–1987
- (Summer Employment) Technical Trainee

1985–1986
- Upgraded failure testing of 100 personal computers and peripherals
- Performed evaluations on software and hardware and made recommendations to management
- Interfaced with vendors and provided technical support for end-users
- Developed relational data base project for computing budget planning

ACHIEVEMENTS:
- Worked 20 hours per week as junior analyst while attending school full-time
- Earned 4.0 GPA in major
- Won President's scholarship

Figure 4.13

Sample Technical Résumé for recent grad. Marginal notes represent manager's comments.

key to your new job. These projects should be significant enough that each can be clearly described in one or two short sentences. Each sentence should begin with a power verb such as one of the following (and see Figure 4.3):

Developed	Analyzed
Designed	Synthesized
Implemented	Evaluated
Simulated	Synchronized
Created	Invented

This section will be followed by your basic résumé components drawn from the basic, draft résumé you prepared at the beginning of this chapter.

Professional Experience

Professional Affiliations

Special Skills

Achievements

Ryan, a programmer and systems analyst, prepared a technical résumé that highlights his strengths quite nicely, even though he's a recent grad with hardly any work experience. His sample résumé (Figure 4.13) provides an excellent model.

Focusing Diverse Experience: The Combination Résumé

Combining the advantage of the chronological, functional, and technical formats in one résumé is a smart move for those who are making a career change and those who have held diverse jobs. It allows you to show off all of your strengths and creatively arrange them, camouflaging any weaknesses. Using the combination format allows you to include everything that will score points for you.

skills summary

grades

accomplishments

job history

other job specific information (such as sideline jobs)

courses/projects

Switching Careers — I found this format most helpful when I coached Brett, a job search client of mine who was going through a career change. Although he had seven years of solid work experience as a teacher, Brett didn't have any experience in business. He was applying for a position as a junior account executive at a Fortune 100 oil company. His challenge was to show that the skills and experience he'd developed as a teacher were relevant to the new position. He knew his skills were very relevant: communication, self-presentation, management/administration, creativity (Figure 4.14). But he also knew that his prospective employer wouldn't see it that way unless he did a superb job of convincing her.

During his job search, Brett had so many doors slammed in his face that he knew the thinking of the interviewers. It went something like this: "How can teaching high school and college English be the least bit relevant to our needs? We need people to sell products to our customers. You've spent your whole life talking to kids about Shakespeare and participles, and that doesn't have anything at all to do with selling oil products." Well, no—it doesn't. But, anyone who understands the skills involved in teaching and the skills that make a good account executive can see the direct correlation. So, Brett knew that his challenge was to graphically illustrate all the skills involved in teaching and put this in a business context. The result was a 4-page combination résumé with the entire first and second pages (Figure 4.14) devoted to a skills summary. I think this format is effective because it is:

- easy to read (wide margins and 1 line per skill)
- detailed and specific
- organized into business related categories

Brett's résumé is shown in Figures 4.14 and 4.15.

Then on the third page, he continued with a chronology of his job history. Beneath each job listing he included four or five accomplishments, using powerful business terms such as these (see Figure 4.3):

designed	supervised
developed	initiated
organized	edited
analyzed	selected
evaluated	implemented
managed	established

Focusing Diverse Experience – Over a period of about twelve years, Joan had changed jobs five times and had worked in three different

Brett Blake
123 Evergreen Drive
Anywhere, USA 12345
123-456-7890

CAREER OBJECTIVE:
Junior Account Executive

critical skill in sales → PROFESSIONAL SKILLS SUMMARY

Communication

Skilled in:
- Group dynamics
- Managing diverse personalities
- All facets of English grammar, writing, and literature
- Instructing adults in composition with emphasis on organizing ideas and critical thought
- Development and teaching of reading and study skills, including motivation techniques, time and stress management
- Planning and conducting workshops, seminars, discussions, and briefings
- Editing, public speaking, technical writing, planning and chairing effective meetings
- Coordinating and individualizing groups
- Committee Work

key skills in sales →

Administration/Management

Skilled in:
- Supervising teachers, tutorial assistants, and editorial staff
- Interviewing, screening, and training personnel
- Performance feedback techniques
- Control of department finances
- Design and implementation of new programs

Brett Blake

    Development and administration of resources center
    Assessment and improvement of morale
    Development of in-service workshops to improve performance
    Evaluation of ability, growth, and performance
    Counseling and disciplinary action *— important for success in selling*
    Productivity improvement

Creativity
Skilled in:
    Design and maintenance of motivational atmosphere
    Development of innovative programs to stimulate ideas, creativity, and awareness
    Design exercises to increase instructional relevance
    Design and conduct courses and workshops in adult self-improvement
    Initiating and publishing school and corporate newspapers, magazines, and yearbooks.
    Establishment, administration, and evaluation of innovative programs for enrichment activities
    Organization of goal-oriented programs and putting ideas into action
    Problem identification and resolution

Figure 4.14
Sample skills summary for combination format (career switch from teaching to business.) Marginal notes represent recruiter's comments.

Brett Blake

PROFESSIONAL EXPERIENCE

UNIVERSITY OF SOUTHERN ACME, Anywhere, USA
Lecturer English (9/84–Present)
- Develop, instruct, and evaluate upper-division English and communication courses.
- Supervise, evaluate, and manage four tutorial assistants, consistently high student ratings.

UNIVERSITY OF ACME, Anywhere, USA
Lecturer (9/86–Present)
- Develop, instruct, and evaluate business writing courses.
- Developed four new courses and a certificate. Student ratings were consistently 8.8 out of 9.0.

WEST ACME UNIVERSITY, Anywhere, USA
Director, Professional Programs
(1/84–Present)
- Recruit, supervise, and evaluate team of six to ten instructors.
- Direct university degree programs for undergraduates, graduates, and professionals.
- Developed nine new courses and a certificate program. Doubled sales for two consecutive years. Student ratings were consistently 3.8 out of 4.0.

ACME STATE UNIVERSITY, Anywhere, USA
Instructor of Business Writing (9/81–5/84)
- Develop and instruct, evaluate communication courses with emphasis on critical and analytical thinking.
- Consistently high student ratings.

Brett Blake

ACME HIGH, Anywhere, USA
Department Chairperson
- Supervise and evaluate instructors and teaching assistants.
- Manage all facets of departmental administration, including management of budget, evaluation of teacher performance, and curriculum effectiveness.
- Organize and administer learning resources center, department library, and audio-visual materials.
- Initiate and manage Literary Society, Literary Magazine, and Drama Society.
- Create department handbook and chairperson job description, including self-evaluation.

SPECIAL ACHIEVEMENTS
- Designed and launched new products for Acme College.
- Publish bimonthly column for ABC Scholastic Journal.
- Won the ACME State Scholarship for undergraduate study.
- Earned all expenses through undergraduate and graduate school with scholarships and part-time work.

EDUCATION
Acme Community Colleges, INSTRUCTOR CREDENTIAL, No. 123456, 1977
University of Acme, Anywhere, USA, MASTER OF ARTS, ENGLISH, 1975
Acme College, Anywhere, USA, BACHELOR OF ARTS, ENGLISH, 1973. 4.0 GPA in major

Figure 4.15: Sample Combination Résumé for career switch

fields. Her challenge was to find a common thread that could link her diverse experience in a dental office, insurance company, and medical office. Her solution (Figure 4.16) worked well for her, and it was effective for a number of reasons:

concise, multi-option objective

detailed qualifications

accomplishments organized by business

job history shows steady employment

Joan's résumé presents her complicated work history in a clear, well-organized format.

Once you've got some experience under your belt in a selected area, it's smart to highlight this with an **Experience Summary** at the top of your résumé. This is different than the Skills Summary discussed earlier which highlights skill areas. The Experience Summary gives total years of experience. With nearly twenty years in the work force Gwen, a communications manager for a large diet products firm, can use an experience summary to her advantage because it allows her to group quasi-related experiences, creating a more focused career path and enhancing her image as a seasoned professional (Figure 4.17).

Once you've got some experience under your belt, total years can be impressive. This format allowed Gwen to highlight 41 years experience. This strategy is designed to downplay the fact that she job hopped reporter, librarian, and convention coordinator for several years. Because some of this experience no longer seemed relevant, she

---

EXPERIENCE SUMMARY

Seventeen years in corporate management and communication

Ten years in management development at ABC International

Seven years as Manager of Professional Development

Five years as Communication Specialist

Two years publishing monthly column in West Coast Journal of Business and Management

Figure 4.17

Multi-objective for multi-skills background

Joan Dee
123 Lemon Lane
Anywhere, USA 12345
123-456-7890

OBJECTIVE: Office Management—Medical Practice Management—Consulting

QUALIFICATIONS—SPECIAL SKILLS
- Experienced manager of dental and medical practices and clinics
- Broad background in practice development, patient/client services, coordination and development of leasehold services, and facility management
- Solid experience in fee definition, billing, collections, medical and dental insurance, Medicare and MediCal
- Excellent record of recruiting, hiring, employee development, and staff management
- Enthusiastic problem solver with a positive, mature attitude, excelling in planning and preparation
- Good communication skills and the flexibility to coordinate office goals

ACCOMPLISHMENTS—DENTAL
- Managed a wide variety of dental practices in various clinical settings
- Managed in-house lab control, financial arrangements, case presentations, facilitation and follow-up of dental and medical insurances and prepaid plans
- Supervised the opening of a corporate dental clinic, including coordination of the leasehold improvements, staffing, and

> Joan Dee
>
> > effectively integrating the corporate systems into efficient administrative policies and actions
> > - Supervised and managed a staff of 12, including dentists, dental assistants, and front office staff
>
> ACCOMPLISHMENTS—MEDICAL
> - Account Manager and Department Manager for a national medical practice management company handling accounts in excess of $1BB
> - Managed medical and psychiatric accounts for clients in university settings, including billing, collections, and practice management
> - Facilitated account management through interaction with other departments in the company
> - Supervised and managed a staff of 15, including account auditors, prebilling clerks, and file clerks
>
> 2 of 2

Figure 4.16: Sample Combination Format Marginal notes represent employers comments.

needed to find a way of grouping it with something else (management) and creating a focus that fits with her current career goals (corporate management and communication). Be careful though—you don't want to arouse suspicion by trying to hide or conceal something major in your background. What you want to do is downplay or de-emphasize irrelevant experiences which you feel will work against you. This can be accomplished by combining them with other more relevant experiences and giving the item a broader name; reducing it to a single one-line item and burying it among other more interesting items. For example, Gwen downplayed her experience job hopping by reducing it to the last entry in her professional experience list (see Figure 4.18) under the heading of communication. So, her Experience

Summary ties it all together and focuses a solid professional base in two related areas:

corporate management

communication

Gwen's résumé highlights this strategy in Figure 4.19.

This format works well for the seasoned professional. The experience summary highlights years of experience (10 years in management). It can be followed by a skills summary which highlights skill areas (such as program design or computer skills) and/or work history, as well as the other basic résumé components.

Tom wanted to downplay his job hopping experience when he switched to a career in electronics sales so, he effectively combined three jobs over a five year period into one entry. The hiring manager told me he thought this approach works well.

The trick is to reword, carefully emphasizing advantages and downplaying less relevant experience. The issue probably won't come up in the interview because it's not very relevant. But, if it does, you should be honest. Remember to plan for this while writing your résumé and don't include anything you couldn't defend in the interview.

(This downplays 5 years of job-hopping at various companies by grouping them as a single item.)

COMMUNICATION

Central City Corporations (9/75–7/80)

Wrote, edited and organized various types of information for the public.

Figure 4.18: Example of Downplaying Less Relevant Experience

GIVING YOUR RÉSUMÉ A POLISHED APPEARANCE

Before sending out your résumé, you must make sure that it's absolutely perfect. It's critical that you maintain the same high quality in appearance that you have in composing your tailored résumé. A poor appearance will always work against you! Managers who are reviewing a high volume of applications often won't even consider poor-looking résumés, and many have told me they won't review anything that's sloppy or that has spelling and grammar errors.

Select stationery and envelopes. Remember, it doesn't need to be

Gwen Brown
123 Palm Lane
Anywhere, USA 12345
123-456-7890

CAREER OBJECTIVE: Director of Training and Development for small company or Senior Staff Position at large corporation.

EXPERIENCE SUMMARY
- Seventeen years in corporate management and communication
- Ten years in management development at ABC International
- Seven years as Manager of Professional Development
- Five years communication specialist
- Two years publishing bimonthly column in *West Acme Journal of Business and Management*

PROFESSIONAL EXPERIENCE

MANAGEMENT ASSOCIATION, Anywhere, USA
Manager, Professional Development
(10/91–Present)
Won "Board of Directors Award" for Outstanding Performance.
- Supervise and evaluate a team of 25 instructors.
- Develop Interpersonal Skills Certificate—a series of ten 10-hour courses.
- Manage Professional Development Program (over 100 courses per year conducted evenings and weekends).
- Responsible for new course development and evaluation of new courses.
- Manage scheduling and budget. Produce 50-page annual catalog.

Gwen Brown

ABC INTERNATIONAL, Anywhere, USA
Management Specialist (9/89–9/91)
Won "Suggestion Award" for contribution to department goals.
- Work directly with executive staff planning and organizing training for division business strategies.
- Develop annual training plan and budget.
- Work directly with upper management to determine and address the organization's corporate culture and needs.
- Conduct company-wide assessments of training needs and training effectiveness.
- Work through functional centers of excellence to establish consulting projects aimed at organizational change.
- Implemented annual $18K cost savings.

Educational Programs Administrator
(2/88–9/89)
Won award for outstanding contribution to productivity.
- Assume lead role in designing and organizing core management courses.
- Develop and manage integrated, cost-effective programs for management development (100 courses involving 25 instructors and more than 1,000 students).
- Manage program budget of more than $1MM annually.
- Implemented annual $40K cost savings.
- Counsel employees regarding appropriate course of study at college level; recruit, screen, and evaluate qualified instructors for professional development course.

Gwen Brown

Promoted to Management Specialist
Human Resources Specialist (1/83–2/88)
Won Department Award for outstanding performance.
- Design and present management and professional development courses.
- Train and supervise 30 instructors for cross-functional employee development programs.
- Design integrated systems for scheduling, tracking, and administering developmental programs involving 7,500 employees.
- Doubled enrollment two years in a row.

Promoted to
Educational Programs Administrator
CENTRAL CITY CORPORATIONS,
Anywhere, USA
Communication Specialist (9/77–12/82)
- Wrote, edited, and organized various types of information for the public.

PROFESSIONAL AFFILIATIONS:
- National Society of Corporate Trainers
- Management Association—Speakers Bureau

SPECIAL SKILLS:
- Public Speaking
- Lotus 1-2-3
- Microsoft Word

ACHIEVEMENTS:
- Completed requirements for Certified Managers Exam. Will take exam 1/92.

> Gwen Brown
>
> - Earned 100 percent expenses through undergraduate and graduate school.
> - Write monthly column for *ABC Journal of Training and Development.*
>
> EDUCATION:
> - M.A., Management, Acme University, Anywhere, USA
> - B.A., Human Resource Management, Acme University, Anywhere, USA (3.8 GPA)

Figure 4.19: Sample Combination Résumé for a seasoned professional

expensive. Look for a matching set in conservative professional tones such as white, beige, grey, or light blue. Employers are not influenced by cost. Inexpensive personalized stationery using black or brown ink is an excellent option.

Choose your printing method. Your options include offset (most expensive), typewriter (least expensive), laser printer (moderately priced). I recommend the word processor for its crisp, professional look and easy update. If you don't have one available, a typewriter is fine.

Hire a typist. If you're not an excellent typist yourself, this is a MUST and a worthwhile investment. Center your name, address, and phone number at the top of page one. Make sure your margins are at least one inch on both sides. You'll never get a second chance to make a good first impression if your typing doesn't present you as a polished professional.

Select appropriate type. Meet with your typist and discuss your typeface options. In addition to considering the appropriate size, it's a good idea to also consider style. A script style, for example, isn't as businesslike and sharp as some of the other letter styles. Don't let the size of your letters get too small. This makes reading difficult and might discourage a prospective boss. If you're typing your own résumé, always make sure that your keys are clean and your ribbon is dark enough to create a crisp professional document.

Proofread your résumé carefully. If possible, use software editing for tips on spelling, grammar, punctuation, vocabulary, and format. If you don't have access to such software, get a partner—a respected colleague to help proofread errors. Working with a partner on this is a must. If you have time, it's a good idea to circulate your résumé among your colleagues and ask for feedback.

Make required corrections and proofread again. This is one document that's got to be absolutely flawless before it goes out.

Arrange for reproduction. Decide how many copies you'll want to send out now and add a few more to this number so that you can follow up on any new leads immediately.

COMMON QUESTIONS ABOUT RÉSUMÉS

Should I keep my résumé to one page?

I think this is the most frequently asked résumé question. It's a controversial issue that leaves many people in a real dilemma. They've been advised by so-called experts (career counselors and such) that going to two pages is suicidal. This may be good advice for some recent grads to keep them from going overboard with irrelevant material, but it certainly doesn't apply in all cases. My advice is this: *Do what works best for you.* If you have experience, skills, and achievements that will help to qualify you for a particular job and set you apart from the crowd, by all means include everything. If that takes you to two pages—so what? That's better than trying to crowd everything onto one page, making it difficult to read. After reading this chapter, you'll know how to keep your ideas concise and focused, so you won't need to be concerned about length. Résumés printed on both sides of the paper are frowned upon by most professional recruiters.

Should I include hobbies/activities and interests?

This is another controversial area. Many experts say that including hobbies and activities makes you seem well-rounded. I think it's risky because your reader's preferences and biases are unknown. And why take an unnecessary risk? Listing your hobbies and interests isn't required and it doesn't contribute anything to your qualifications for the job. I see two risks involved here. First, the manager can draw unfair conclusions based on hobbies. One applicant, a telecommunications specialist at a medium size manufacturing firm, listed seemingly harmless interests such as swimming, skiing, tennis, and sailing which aroused suspicions in the manager that he wasn't a team player (where's the basketball and football?); or a concern that this applicant won't want to work overtime for fear of missing the action sports.

The second risk is the unknown bias. For example, I know one manager who thinks all motorcyclists are wild and crazy outlaws. What chance would a motorcycle enthusiast have in his department? There are exceptions. When your hobby is closely related to your job skills, then it's a plus that could help qualify you for the job. If, for instance, you're like my colleague, Christine, a computer designer for a small firm who also builds computer hybrids as a hobby, you should definitely include your hobby.

Will including a photo or artwork help to distinguish me?

Yes, it will distinguish you in most industries because this is generally not done. However, it won't distinguish you for your qualifications. This is an extravagant expense that could work against you, particularly if the successful applicant will be required to control a tight budget. Another risk here has to do with personal bias. Under the Affirmative Action laws, it's illegal for an employer to discriminate on the basis of appearance. We know, however, that we can't legislate bias from a manager's mind. And people have many different kinds of biases, often on an unconscious level.

Should I list promotions?

This is an excellent way to distinguish yourself as an achiever who has made valuable contributions to your employer's goals. Conspicuously listing your promotion under your position description works well. It also fits well in the achievements section, particularly if you were promoted quickly or if you were distinguished for something, such as being the youngest person or the only intern ever to hold this position.

Should I include personal information, and are there any other creative résumé tricks I can use to deal with employer bias?

Unfortunately, there are many different kinds of bias alive and well in the workplace. In addition to age, race, and religion there are biases relating to sex, people with children, people without children, single people, the handicapped, smokers, non-smokers, tall people, short people, overweight people, thin people, re-entry women, and an endless array of biases that have nothing to do with your ability to get the job done.

Dealing effectively with these biases can be difficult but there are a few simple steps you can take to minimize the damage:

    a) Deal only with job-relevant information on your résumé. Keep everything else close to the vest. The chapter on interviews explains how to handle these issues if they come up in the interview.

You can creatively arrange your résumé to conceal any information that you think could work against you—even something as basic as your sex. I know one woman who protected herself against sex discrimination at the résumé stage by changing her first name to Cameron, which could also be a man's name. I know many women who use initials instead of a first name for this same reason.

    b) Present your qualifications so impressively that they will overcome any bias by convincing the employer that you're absolutely perfect for the job.

I've seen people include their age, height, weight, sexual preference, health, their spouse's age, height, weight; and even their children's ages and education! One applicant, an attorney for a small firm, even included the fact that in her spare time she gives small dinner parties and raises three children. These people are giving away too much information, which is bad for business and risky. There's room for every type of judgmental conclusion and bias to have free play here. Unless she's in the catering business, the applicant who uses her spare time to give dinner parties isn't contributing to her professional image. The boss might see her as lacking commitment to the job. And her equating children with spare time and dinner parties could leave the reader wondering about the values of a mother who trivializes child rearing in such a way. The best guideline is to include only job-relevant information. Some jobs do have physical requirements (fireman, policeman, airline pilot, fashion model), and these should be included on the résumé. Otherwise, for most jobs, all personal information should be kept confidential.

Should I mention willingness to travel/relocate?

This is usually handled better in the interview, so I recommend leaving it off. If, however, you know that these are requirements of the job, it will help you in presenting yourself as the perfect fit, so use it.

Will it be an advantage to state that I'm a non-smoker?

As more and more communities legislate against smoking in public places, non-smokers are gaining an advantage in many workplaces.

There is a risk, however. If your prospective boss is a chain smoker, he or she may take your declaration to mean that you're intolerant of smokers, and this will work against you. For this reason, I recommend leaving this issue for the interview (if it comes up).

I've heard that it's acceptable (and even expected) to lie about your salary on your résumé. Is this true?

Never lie about anything. In one way or another, it will always come back to haunt you. My advice is simple—fluff, yes; lie, no! Let me explain. In some industries it's acceptable to augment or "fluff," your base salary by adding in extra income such as the value of benefits, perks, bonuses, and so on, but you need to be careful here. You could price yourself out of the running. And you could risk losing your credibility. Many companies require you to document your salary with a recent pay stub or income tax return. This could put you in the awkward position of trying to justify your claim.

My advice on the issue of salary is to let *them* make the first move. Don't include it on your résumé unless it's specified in the ad. Even then, you need to do some probing before disclosure. If possible, try calling to ask the salary range. Carolyn, an industrial engineer for a medium size engineering firm, once called about a job that sounded perfect, only to learn that the top of the salary range was $15,000 less than her current salary. This call saved her a lot of time. She didn't need to bother applying at that firm.

Salary negotiations are usually handled at the second interview. (There will be more on how to handle this discussion in Chapter 7, "The Interview".)

If I'm still working on my degree or professional certificate, can I include this on my résumé?

Yes, you definitely want to include everything that will enhance your qualifications. Further education is always a plus if it's in the right field closely related to your job. So, how do you go about including your education in process? If you're more than halfway through the program, simply list your degree or certificate objective, your major or areas of specialization, and your expected graduation date (month and year) under the education category on your résumé.

When you're less than halfway through, it's more impressive to list areas of specialization and specific job-related courses you've completed. You can enhance this by including your GPA if you feel it's impressive (3.0 and above). This information profiles a serious commitment to achieving your educational and professional goals.

Should I list references?

Listing references on your résumé is unnecessary. If references are required, the employer will probably request them either on the application form or in the interview. Many experts recommend including a statement at the bottom of your résumé indicating that references are available on request. However, I feel this is unnecessary. It's assumed that if you want the job, you'll provide excellent references on request.

Is it necessary to fill out an application when you're submitting a résumé?

Although it seems redundant (and I know applications can be a real pain to fill out), many companies do require an application, for various reasons. Having the same data on all applicants on a standard form simplifies the review process. It makes it easier for the reviewer to pinpoint specific information. Application forms also ensure that the employer gets all the information their company needs such as: social security number, driver's license number, salary history, address, phone number, and references' names. So, when you're applying as a walk-in and when you go to your interview, it's a good idea to have all this information with you.

An application generally provides more detailed information than the résumé does. If you have your résumé with you when filling out your application, you can use the tailored résumé information to present yourself as a perfect fit for the job.

Before filling out an application it's a good idea to review your affirmative action rights. To protect your rights, legislation makes it illegal for an employer to ask certain questions in the hiring process. You are not required to disclose any information regarding personal issues such as physical characteristics, family, age, race, religion, or sex. Call your local state employment office to request information on these laws. If the application asks you an illegal question, or any question you don't want to answer, you can leave it blank.

Must I include dates on my résumé?

This is an interesting question, and how you decide to handle it depends on your objectives.

Certainly, you want to include on your résumé only those items that will work to your advantage. If you suspect that your age may work against you, then you don't have to give it away. By law, employers are not allowed to ask about your age during the employment process. However, dates on a résumé (particularly of graduation and first job) can be a dead giveaway. If the employer is looking for someone younger or older than you are, this could lose the interview for you.

If you have all the right qualifications and they're presented creatively on your résumé, you'll get called for an interview. In the interview, you'll have the chance to use your personality, warmth, and persuasive skills to overcome any hidden bias on the part of the interviewer.

To avoid arousing suspicions about long absences from the workplace ("was he in prison?"), it's a good idea to account for each year. Employers like to know what you've been doing with yourself. So, if at all possible, you want to provide a chronology for at least the last ten years. This is the conventional way of doing a résumé and most managers expect to see dates. Of course, if you feel this will work against you because of age, as we discussed earlier, dates may be omitted.

Long absences for personal reasons can best be identified as "family business." This looks professional, and it certainly legitimizes your absence. If the issue comes up in the interview, you can always add detail then, and it probably won't work against you.

So, if you're worried about age discrimination or absence from the job market, a dateless résumé may be the answer; you can simply list number of years at each job, as a 56-year-old housewife who had just graduated did in her résumé (Figure 4.12).

Should I use a colorful folder to make my résumé stand out?

Your qualifications, not gimmicks or cosmetics, are what will distinguish you. A poorly prepared résumé in a fancy cover won't get you anywhere, but a well-tailored résumé that is professionally presented will get attention. This is true in most industries.

That said, however, there are some industries such as the arts, entertainment, and advertising where your ability to be innovative can speak volumes about your qualifications. My business students from advertising firms have shared some rather remarkable stories with me about bizarrely presented résumés that won the job. One was written on onion skin rolled up inside a walnut. Another was in the shape of a shoe, and the only way to read it was to hold it upside down in front of a mirror. Bizarre, but true! The guideline is "Know your industry!"

Is it a good idea to include lists of professional accomplishments such as courses taught?

In some industries, such as entertainment, listing the projects you've worked on is the central focus of your résumé. In most industries, however, the central focus will be skills and job history.

I recommend including your list of special accomplishments on a separate page at the end of your résumé, as a sort of addendum. Eileen, an applicant I interviewed for a training specialist job a few years ago, did a nice job of this (Figure 4.20). I liked her format because it highlights her diverse teaching skills. At a quick glance, the reviewer can immediately assess her areas of expertise. You can prepare a list to highlight your own industry-specific accomplishments such as publications, research grants, and special projects.

How far back should I go with my job history?
Most employers like to see what you've been doing for the last ten years or so...work, school, family, business, etc. It will be to your advantage to leave out "ancient history" (anything beyond ten years) and jobs that aren't relevant to your current career goals. The part-time jobs I had in college were dropped from my résumé by the time I had a few years of solid professional experience under my belt. The key here is to remember that you're not writing your autobiography. You're only outlining relevant career highlights.

Should I include military experience and honorable discharge?
Include military experience only if it provides relevant career qualifications or some other relevant information. For example, a young person with no other work history would want to include military experience to show maturity, discipline, and perseverance.

Do managers have pet peeves when reviewing résumés?
Managers that I've talked to over the years all complain about the same things:

- *carelessness*—typos, misspellings, punctuation and grammar errors
- *extraneous information*—hobbies, personal information, social or religious organizations
- *trite career objectives*—your career enhancement doesn't interest employers
- *poor appearance*—reading through dense, single-spaced prose with narrow margins is a turn-off
- *no phone number*—failing to supply your phone number is not the fastest way to get an interview
- *too small print*—trying to squeeze three pages of information onto a single sheet makes for difficult reading

Eileen Shaw: Courses designed and taught

MANAGEMENT DEVELOPMENT

- Challenging Employees to Succeed
- Communications for Managers
- Effective Meetings
- Ethics and Standards of Business
- First Line Management
- Leadership and Strategic Thinking
- Meeting Leadership
- Managing for Success
- Management Practices
- Managing Assertively
- Negotiation Skills
- Organizational Behavior (graduate level)
- Professional Skills
- Principles of Management
- Pre-Supervisory Skills
- Productivity Improvement
- Skills of Managing
- Strategic Leadership
- Technical Information Management
- Team Building and Conflict Resolution
- Time Management for Managers
- The Effective Professional Manager

SELF-MANAGEMENT

- Assertiveness Training
- Creative Thinking
- Career Planning
- Conflict Resolution and Team Building
- Creative Problem Solving and Decision Making
- Everything is Negotiable
- Image Skills
- Managing Retirement
- Memory Improvement
- Networking
- Organization and Goal Setting
- Peak Performance
- Psychology of Success
- Personal Productivity
- Professional Development for Instructors
- Stress Management
- Time Management
- Women in Business
- Working with People

MANAGEMENT COMMUNICATION

- Business Communication (graduate)
- Business Writing
- Business Communication (undergraduate)
- Clear Writing

> (Management communication, cont'd.)
> Communicating for Success
> Foundation Skills of Business Writing
> Letters and Reports
> Proposal Writing
> Professional Communication Skills
> Résumé Writing
> Writing with Punch
> Writing Procedure
> Communication for Managers
> Specialized Business Writing Strategies
> Technical Writing Strategies
> Technical Writing for Scientists
> Technical Writing for Engineers

Figure 4.20: Sample addendum adds detail to résumé.

Figures 4.21–4.23 are samples of poorly prepared résumés with marginal notes indicating the manager's reaction. In tough times managers often discard carelessly prepared résumés as a way of weeding out the applicants.

As a result of a corporate merger I was downgraded from director to manager. Is there any way to effectively conceal this on my résumé without lying?

Yes, there is! With some clever maneuvering you can present even the most unfortunate situation in a positive light. To accomplish this, you'll need to use a modified chronological format.

Duane's sample provides an excellent model (Figure 4.24). He listed total years with the corporation, but did not include dates with each position. This allowed him to creatively camouflage the demotion by listing his director position first. So, it appears that he has progressed in increasingly more responsible positions. During the interview, if the issue comes up, he can explain the situation truthfully. In the interview, he will have time to sell himself on other points as described in the next chapter. And the downgrade won't be an issue.

Is it possible to present one career with two or three different résumés when applying for different jobs?

This strategy works well for an individual who is multi-skilled or who has cultivated a sideline that can be converted to a core career. Dan, a stock analyst at a bank who developed computer expertise, is a good example. Developing a résumé to highlight his banking experience would work well if he stayed in that industry. On the other

KAREN LEE
123 Chestnut Road
Anywhere, USA 12345

not specific   CAREER OBJECTIVE: Software Development

EDUCATION: Acme University, Anywhere, USA
B. S., Computer Science, 1980

is this a certificate? date of completion

Acme University Extension
Relational Database Technology

SKILLS: Programming Languages: C, JOVIAL, Pascal, Ada, BASIC, 1750A

Computer Systems: VAX 8350, 780, Micro, Station; IBM PC, Macintosh

Operating Systems: VAX/VMS, DOS, UNIX

Software: MacDraw/Write/Paint, ALL-IN-1, VAX C, DEC VAX/CMS, WPS-PLUS, VAX Rdb/VMS, Datatrieve, Turbo C, Microsoft Word, VolksWriter, ACT JOVIAL J73, Systems GSID, General Dynamics 1750 A Simulator

EXPERIENCE:

dates are buried

MEMBER OF TECHNICAL STAFF,
ABC International, 1982

narration is hard to read

Member Controller project Software Support Tools Team. Designed and developed a relational database Change Tracking System tool for use in tracking software problems. Wrote various general-purpose utility programs utilizing VAX C, DEC system service routines, RMS, and file applications.

Karen Lee

SOFTWARE ENGINEER,
XYZ Electronics, 1980–1982

Developed beam correction, jammer identification software for the operational flight program of the Advanced Identification system. Utilized Macintosh for generation of data flow diagrams and detailed flowcharts. Wrote code, software documentation, and test cases on the VAX. Participated in customer reviews. Established software engineering department standards and procedures. Provided training for VAX and Macintosh.

INSTRUCTOR, Private Consultant,
1982–Present

Tutored and instructed new users on the IBM PC. Topics include introduction to the IBM PC, DOS, and Microsoft Word.

not needed

PERSONAL BACKGROUND: U. S. Citizen

REFERENCES: Available upon request.

INTERESTS: Swimming, Skiing, Sailing

Figure 4.21: Sample of Weak Format

Richard Ross
123 Strawberry Lane
Anywhere, USA
123-456-7890

needs career objective

PROFESSIONAL EXPERIENCE:

1970–Present ABC Inc., Anywhere, USA
STAFFING ADVISOR

need more quantifiable data

Responsible for recruitment of technical, professional, and data processing positions at corporate and field locations. Assist with EEO recruitment, employee counseling, exit interviews. Assist with special employment related projects including job fairs, recruitment brochures and college recruiting.

HUMAN RESOURCES SPECIALIST
Recruited for exempt and non-exempt positions. Organized and presented weekly employee orientation programs. Coordinated temporary employee program.

EMPLOYEE REPRESENTATIVE
Recruited for non-exempt positions. Designed and implemented evaluation program for clerical applicants.

too vague & doesn't add anything

1965–1970 Acme Unified School District, Anywhere, USA
TEACHER
Taught various subjects at the elementary level.

EDUCATION: B. A. Liberal Arts
Acme Multiple Subjects Teaching Credential
Acme University, Anywhere, USA

Figure 4.22: Sample of weak format

NAME: Nancy Thomas
TITLE: Text Processing Specialist

ABC International, 1974–Present:
Specific Duties:

Train personnel on the Multimate system, including:
> Basic Word Processing Concepts—the screen, the keyboard, creating and editing documents, using document index, and printing a document.
>
> Intermediate Word Processing—formatting text (using a Multimate ruler, revising format lines, horizontal scroll, using format keys, formatting, columns of text, creating pages); text editing (strikeover, delete, insert, replace, adjusting page length); copying and moving text.
>
> Advanced Word Processing—centering headings over columns; text attributes (underscore, double underscore, strike through, boldface, superscript, and subscript); stop codes; hyphenating text; paginating text; creating headers and footers; making operator notes.

Other Functions
> Document filing (filing to/archiving from, recovering, and duplicating archive diskettes); dual column print, document merge, sorting; glossary (creating, attaching, and recalling glossary entries).

too much text

Nancy Thomas

    Specialized applications such as layout of formal tables and typing equations.

    Create and update the Word Processing Manual, writing and/or changing procedures, formats, and job aids as required.

    Handle day-to-day questions from word processors on correct procedures to ensure standardization and consistency.

    Coordinate, proof, edit, and type a variety of documents on the Multimate system.

Administrative Duties:

hard to read   Responsible for maintaining a dual system which consists of two Office Information Systems. Responsibilities include initializing and updating the system disks, updating software, performing backup, telecommunicating documents to other remote Wang systems, and solving users' problems.

    Create glossaries which store information for later use such as frequently used words, phrases, and standard paragraphs.

    Program the system using Decision Processing to perform predetermined tasks, sequences, and entire operations, which increases the sophistication of glossary entries.

Figure 4.23: Sample of Weak Format

Duane Dawson
123 Nutberry Lane
Anywhere, USA 12345
123-456-7890

listing total years experience de-emphasizes downgrade

PROFESSIONAL EXPERIENCE
Operations Management, ABC International, Anywhere, USA
June 1965 to June 1986

leaving off dates allows you to put higher level experience at top

Director of Widget Engineering
Acme Division

- Organize, manage, and direct professional managers and their subordinates in budgeting, funding, designing, constructing, operating, and maintaining all widgets.

- Established appropriation and control of the group's capital budget and participation in the development of the group's strategic business plan.

Manager of Widget Engineering, XYZ Division

- Organize, manage, and direct professional managers and their subordinate engineers in providing Widget Engineering Services to XYZ Division.

ACHIEVEMENTS:
Recipient "Engineering Merit Award," ABC Engineer's Council

Commendation, National Association of Professional Engineers

Fellow, Institute for the Advancement of Engineering

> Duane Dawson
>
> PROFESSIONAL AFFILIATIONS:
> Past President, Widget Engineering Association
>
> Member, Board of Directors, Greater ABC Transportation Coalition
>
> Member, President's Advisory Council, Acme State University
>
> EDUCATION:
> Bachelor of Science, Widget Engineering, University of Acme
> Anywhere, USA
>
> Registered Professional Engineer

Figure 4.24: Dateless Sample to camouflage demotion

hand, if he wanted to market himself as a computer expert, he would develop a separate résumé highlighting his computer expertise. The basic chronological format might be a good choice for presenting a core banking career in which he's advanced over the years. A functional, technical, or combination format might be a better choice when trying to establish himself as a computer expert.

Now that you've prepared your basic marketing tools, the cover letter and résumé, you're ready to go beyond the basics and develop other marketing materials in Chapter 5.

> As you complete the chapter on The Well Crafted Résumé: Tailoring Your Qualifications, you should have filed the following items in your **Job Search Notebook** (in addition to a page for each of the five basic résumé categories specified at the beginning of Chapter 4).
>
> Lists of volunteer experiences and skills, learned in school, or through home management
>
> List converting above experiences to job qualifications
>
> Draft résumé—chronological format
>
> Final résumé in your tailored format

CHAPTER 5

Beyond the Basics: Other Marketing Materials

"It's not what you are that holds you back, it's what you think you are not."

—*Denis Waitley*

THE RECOMMENDATION PORTFOLIO

As many companies downsize in these tough economic times, hiring the right person—that is, one who has with a high degree of initiative and productivity potential—is critical to employers. How can you show employers you're that person? Developing a recommendation portfolio can be a terrific way for you to get ahead of your competition and showcase your initiative.

The recommendation portfolio is a powerful and persuasive tool. If the letters are well written and customized for your particular job and qualifications, they can set you apart from equally well-qualified applicants. Most managers would agree that a candidate who is confident and resourceful enough to prepare a portfolio brings valuable assets, such as initiative and creativity, to the job. The portfolio makes it clear that this individual goes above and beyond the normal requirements. I was very impressed when a candidate for a training specialist position produced a binder full of recommendations and commendation letters from previous jobs. Although he had less experience than other candidates, such a testimonial to his performance was hard to ignore. And since none of the other applicants submitted anything like this, it really distinguished this inexperienced candidate as a real go-getter.

The key to an effective recommendation is a focused request. Requesting a recommendation is also a good way to begin organizing your skills and experience around an employer's requirements. You will be contacting someone who is familiar with your achievements and qualifications. But that's not enough. You need to provide a guide for the writer which will help him or her sort through everything they know about you and produce a letter highlighting exactly what you can do for your prospective employer. A skillfully crafted request will elicit a targeted and powerful assessment of your ability to do a specific job. So, writing the requests for recommendations can be as important as composing your résumé and should be handled with as much care.

Before you begin composing your request letter, you'll need to do two things:

> decide whom to ask for recommendations
>
> identify what skills and characteristics you want the writer to comment on

Barbara, one of my résumé workshop participants, was a graduating senior preparing for her first job search when she attended my workshop. Months later, Barbara called to let me know that she'd used this strategy and received tailor-made recommendations which won her the job of her dreams.

Whom to ask for a recommendation—Anyone who is familiar with your character and your work is a potential source for a credible evaluation. In addition to previous bosses, you can contact

> higher level boss
>
> mentor
>
> teacher
>
> department chairperson
>
> client
>
> colleague
>
> volunteer committee member
>
> club leader
>
> community leader
>
> coach
>
> clergyman

Never request a recommendation from a subordinate. This lacks credibility.

To begin the process of identifying references, establish a section in your Job Search Notebook under section 5 for recommendations. On the first page you can brainstorm a list of everyone you know who is familiar with your abilities. Be creative. Remember, this is brainstorming, so list as many as you can think of. Try to keep your list relatively current. Ancient references (anything beyond five years or so) have a tendency to lose credibility. Once you have a good list, you can go through and highlight the top ten. If your goal is to get three or four letters, it's a good idea to request ten, just in case some don't respond. Having more responses than you need will also give you the option of weeding out any letters that you feel aren't hitting the mark. Now you're ready to track down your top ten references and record their current addresses in your Job Search Notebook.

When your experience is limited, a good way to build your list of potential sources is to work on volunteer projects. Civic groups such as the Rotary Club, Kiwanis, Junior Achievement, and the YWCA are always looking for a helping hand. In selecting a community service organization it's a good idea to try to find a project or organization that relates in some way to your profession. Also, look for organizations that project credibility. For example, giving a seminar for the Los Angeles County Commission on Human Relations sounds more credible than speaking to the Garden Grove Mom's Club. Frequently, national organizations and government sponsored projects tend to sound more professional (possibly because of their high visibility) than do local groups.

Community service is also a good way to build your experience base and to make valuable contacts while making a contribution to your community. By giving a speech or a seminar in your area of expertise, for example, you may impress a credible community leader who will later be glad to write a letter of recommendation for you. A thank-you letter you receive from an organization can also be used as a reference. A single letter such as this may not be very impressive on its own, but as part of a package, this type of praise builds a winning profile.

Over the years, Gayle, a public relations specialist at a medium-size marketing firm, collected several letters like this (Figures 5.1 and 5.2) and, after reading through them, one manager said she was convinced that Gayle "walks on water"!

Three or four letters together create the profile of an energetic high achiever, full of creativity and commitment—just what employers are looking for in tough times.

One word of caution: before using any letter as a reference, it's important to evaluate it for impact. To be effective, the letter must be well written and letter perfect—no typos or errors. It must be specific about your contribution and the results your work produced. *A poorly written letter will have a negative impact on your credibility.* Figure 5.4 illustrates this point (the names have, of course, been changed to protect the guilty!).

What Should the Letter-Writer Comment On?

Your next step will be to think about what skills and characteristics you want the writer to comment on. Again, brainstorming a list of

---

March 24, 19—
Gayle Anderson
23 Maple Lane
Anywhere, USA 12345

Dear Mrs. Anderson:

On behalf of the 19— Women's Conference Planning Committee, we would like to express our sincere thanks to you for outstanding service as a workshop presenter at our first annual Day for Women on March 7, 19—.

shows emphasis on quality

The contribution of your time and expertise meant a lot to the women of our Valley who attended this event. Your participation helped ensure the success of this first-time event and set a standard of high quality for future conferences.

strong recommendation for leadership

It is because of community leaders like yourself that we can continue to offer such programs. We hope you will be available to work with us in the future. Your dedication is to be commended.

Please accept the enclosed Certificate with our sincere appreciation.

Yours truly,

Jill Smith
Conference Co-Coordinator

Figure 5.1
Strong sample thank-you for community service to be used in recommendation portfolio.

personal characteristics desirable to employers in your Job Search Notebook will be effective in generating ideas. In a competitive job market, I think it's safe to assume that for each open position there will be several technically competent applicants with equal qualifications. If this is the case, then your challenge will be to find a way to distinguish yourself on the basis of non-technical qualifications. Frequently, strong non-technical skills (such as the ability to work

---

April 16, 19—

Gayle Anderson
23 Maple Lane
Anywhere, USA 12345

Dear Gayle:

Thank you so much for your two outstanding and comprehensive presentations on April 1 and April 16. You really helped our marketing team formulate an effective strategy.

detail here adds credibility

I have received nothing but compliments on the organization of your presentations, your presentation style, and your handouts. The managers who attended felt they received inspiration as well as concrete, tangible materials so that they might pursue each topic further.

On behalf of our staff, I thank you again for a job well done!

Sincerely,

June Williams
Acme Marketing Inc.

Figure 5.2
Strong sample thank-you from client to be used for recommendation portfolio.

January 23, 19—
ABC Oil Company
123 Berry Drive
Anywhere, USA 12345

Gentlemen:

As a Business Communication Instructor at Acme University, I'm writing at the request of Anthony Andrews. Anthony asked if I would recommend him for a management trainee position with your firm.

I've known Anthony for about four months. He was a student in my Business Communication Class (X109) at Acme during Fall quarter 19—. In conversations with Anthony, I've been very impressed with his articulate, goal-oriented approach to learning and self-improvement.

Anthony demonstrated considerable initiative in joining my 12-week, 4-unit non-required course on effective writing. This showed considerable commitment on his part. He was willing to put in the extra hours, conscientiously coming to class early with all class assignments carefully prepared. His papers and class participation reflected insight and appreciation for course material. In class, he also demonstrated strong teamwork skills and leadership keeping his group on track during team projects. He worked very hard and earned an "A" in my class.

With 15 years experience teaching undergraduates, graduate students, and professionals, I recognize in Anthony the highly motivated characteristics of a leader: goal-oriented, methodical, and articulate. Although I've only known Anthony for a short time, I feel confident in recommending him for this program.

Sincerely,

Jane Smith

Figure 5.3

Strong recommendation from a professor for a particular position. You may also request a general recommendation to "To whom it may concern" when you're not sure what jobs you'll be applying for.

well with people or to work well under pressure) are so important that a manager will choose someone with these skills over a more technically skilled candidate. As a manager, I would much rather have a secretary with good skills and a highly conscientious approach to her or his work than one with outstanding skills but careless habits and a negative attitude. I once had a secretary who could type 100

October 5, 19—

Paul Baker
123 Kiwi Lane
Anywhere, USA 12345

Dear Paul:

too general — There never seem to be enough ways to say thank you for all the time and energy you have devoted to others. Many young adults' lives have been touched since you made your your high school presentations.

clearly not related to contribution — We don't always see the results of our hard work immediately, but further down the road you will see more informed and resourceful young people.

so what? — The one thing that most impresses me and makes my job worthwhile is that you have volunteered your time to make this all possible. I truly hope that you have gained from this experience and derived your own personal satisfaction. It is my pleasure to be associated with you and hope that we will be in touch for a long time.

Again, thank you for your selfless efforts on behalf of our Free Enterprise System and most importantly our Future Business Leaders.

too friendly — Warmest regards,

Program Manager

Figure 5.4
Sample of weak Thank-You Letter (not appropriate for use in recommendation portfolio).

words per minute. She was an absolute whiz, but her attitude was so negative that she alienated everyone in the department. The secretary I have now only types 65 words per minute but is very enthusiastic and works well with everyone. In today's interdependent world, collaborative skills among employees at all levels are critical to the success of every organization; such skills are therefore important to emphasize in letters of recommendation.

I've prepared a sample list of **Personal Characteristics Desirable to Employers** (Figure 5.5) for you. Pick the ones from this list that most apply to your situation, and add any others that you think are important in your industry.

To get a letter writer to emphasize the specific qualities your potential employer desires requires creativity. You need to carefully avoid asking a recommender to emphasize a particular thing (for example, insight or creativity) and sounding obnoxious. Or worse, implying that the letter-writer can't write a good enough recommendation letter without your input.

Personal Characteristics Desirable to Employers

- enthusiastic
- professional
- skilled with people
- creative
- hard working
- committed
- positive
- intelligent
- skilled at communication
- organized
- efficient
- articulate
- deals well with conflict/difficult people
- insightful
- learns from criticism
- focused
- skilled at setting priorities
- honest
- persuasive
- sales-oriented
- flexible
- ethical
- motivated
- able to do a lot with limited resources
- gets the most from people
- collaborative
- prompt
- works well under pressure
- open to new ideas
- handles multiple priorities
- service oriented
- goal oriented
- team player
- loyal
- industrious
- tactful
- discreet
- confident

Figure 5.5

What works, without risk of arrogance or insult, is to simply state that these are the qualities your prospective job and employer require. Then list six to ten qualities and ask the recommender to comment on your ability in these areas. This works well because it takes the emphasis away from you and places it on the characteristics. It's an objective approach. This is how universities format their recommendation forms, and I've written many recommendations on this basis. I also know from personal experience that this format works because I've had great success with it over the years. This is one of the primary factors that won me a full graduate fellowship. My recommenders (a dozen or so) all commented on how helpful my request letter was in listing specific characteristics. Later, when I used this same technique in business situations, it worked equally well and elicited the same favorable comments from recommenders.

I have shared this technique with my résumé workshop participants, and many successful job seekers have returned to tell me of the beautifully detailed letters of recommendation they received and the positive comments from recommenders on their request letter.

Alan's letter (Figure 5.7) provides an excellent model for your request letter.

How to Write a Request for Recommendation

Before you start writing, you'll need to do some planning and organizing. Hemingway once said "Good writers spend more time planning than they do writing." A few minutes spent in careful planning will save you hours of painful rewriting. It's important in a letter like this to keep it simple. Focus on your purpose, connect with the reader, and get closure, keeping your style crisp and professional. Following the outline in Figure 5.6 will help keep you on track.

Remember to keep the tone of your letter friendly and conversational. You're writing to someone with whom you have a good relationship, so you don't want to sound stiff and formal.

Finally, it's a good idea to include a self-addressed stamped envelope. This makes it easier for your reader and shows that you're thoughtful.

Following this outline will help you get a good response, because you've made it as easy as possible for the recommender, letting him or her know exactly what you want. This format is almost guaranteed to produce an effective recommendation. The sample letters in Figures 5.7 and 5.8 illustrate this point positively, while the letter in Figure 5.9 shows what a disaster lack of planning and asking the wrong evaluator can create.

Alan was one of my business management evening students. He was applying for a graduate fellowship to study journalism and was required to submit five references evaluating his work as well as his character. Alan followed my advice and listed the significant traits he

Outline for Recommendation Request	
Purpose	Explain why you're writing, exactly what you need and what it will be used for. Update the reader on your situation and what's new since you last spoke.
Credibility	Ask the person to include in the letter how he/she knew you. What was your relationship and how long they have known you? (Remind them of these details if you think they may have forgotten.)
Accomplishments	What specific contributions did you make to the organization? What special awards did you earn? Try to quantify accomplishments (i.e. increased sales by a certain percent or implemented cost savings of $__. (Again, don't be afraid to remind them of your work.)
Technical Skill	If appropriate, ask your reader to evaluate your technical skill level (i.e. types 100 wpm with 99 percent accuracy). Don't be afraid to mention the high praise they may have given you in a review.
Personal Characteristics	Choose traits from sample list (Figure 5.5) and ask the reader to comment on these characteristics which you think your prospective employer will be looking for.
Closure	Be sure to thank your reader for his help and give him some idea as to when you'll need a response. Don't be afraid to request a courtesy copy. If the person wants to keep his letter confidential they may do so and you should mention this option when making your request.

Figure 5.6

wanted his references to address. Then he wrote his request letter (Figure 5.7) using my suggested outline.

Alan was pleased with the results. He said the outline helped him to stay focused and concise. With his prepared list of traits, he knew exactly what to ask for, so writing the letter was easy.

He was even more pleased with the response he got from his former boss. The recommendation letter included everything Alan had asked for, and more (Figure 5.8). He was delighted with all of his other recommendations, and he feels these powerful recommendations were critical in his winning the fellowship.

To maintain a good relationship with those who recommended you, it's important to thank them for their letter with a follow-up note or a phone call. Let them know how you're doing—did you get the position, or are you going on to something else? Cultivating these relationships will not only be personally satisfying, but can pay big dividends for your career.

OTHER CREATIVE MARKETING MATERIALS

You may want to pique the employer's interest with a one-page background summary (Figure 5.10) before submitting your résumé. This works well in such situations as consulting, free-lance work, when you're responding to a vague ad, when your submission is unsolicited, and when you already know the employer. Your background summary introduces your qualifications and should be accompanied by a note stating that you'll be happy to send your résumé if desired. The background summary has certain advantages over the résumé. It's simple and easy to read. And with a more flexible structure, it allows you to be very selective in stating only highlights. For example, Susan's background summary (Figure 5.10) doesn't mention job descriptions, but does highlight specific workshops and clients.

Background summaries work well in situations where a résumé is not necessary. For example, as a consultant, Susan doesn't want to tell her clients everything they never wanted to know about her! When they're considering her for a writing or management program, it's unlikely that they'll want to wade through three pages of her job history. Instead, she provides only general information and experience relevant to the type of consulting he'll be doing for the client.

Everyone should have an updated background summary on hand at all times. It will be particularly useful when you're invited to give a speech, submit an article, or give an interview for the media. It can

123 Sycamore Lane
Anywhere, USA 12345
November 10, 19__

Mr. Donald Smith, Editor
Exponent News
Anywhere, USA 12345

Dear Don:

simple & direct

I'm writing to request a letter of recommendation for my application portfolio. As you know, I'm applying for the ABC Graduate Fellowship to study journalism at XYZ next fall.

explains relationship

Working under your expert direction as a staff reporter during the last two summers and Christmas vacations provided a valuable learning experience for me. The Fellowship Committee will be evaluating candidates on very specific criteria. I'd appreciate it very much if you could write a letter commenting on my work in the following areas:

this is roadmap for the recommendation

accomplishments	flexibility
initiative	intelligence
interpersonal skills	efficiency
communication skills	positive attitude
special awards	creativity

friendly thanks

Thank you so much for your help with the recommendation and also for your professional support over the years. I'm including stamped, pre-addressed envelopes to the Fellowship Committee and to me. I'll be submitting my application in about two weeks and recommendations are accepted until December 1.

Thanks again. I'll call you soon to let you know how it's going.

Regards,

Alan Brown

Figure 5.7: Sample letter requesting recommendation

November 17, 19__

Donald L. Smith, Editor
Exponent News
Anywhere, USA 12345

To Whom It May Concern:

It is a pleasure to recommend Mr. Alan Brown for an ABC Graduate Fellowship. He has been one of the most talented, professional, and creative student employees we have ever hired. In fact, he was the only student employee ever to win our prestigious "Rookie Reporter of the Year" award for innovative reporting.

He was employed to fill vacancies during two summer and Christmas vacations, and this arrangement resulted in his assignment to both desk and reporter capacities, posts that he filled well. He accepted all assignments cheerfully, although many of them were difficult night-reporting tasks, and the results of his interviews and reporting were outstanding. I often assigned him to banquets and public meetings, and I found that he was liked by all persons with whom he came into contact. He writes well, regardless of the type of assignment, and on numerous occasions he did special feature work for us.

Mr. Brown is a very intelligent person. He is pleasant and has a keen sense of humor, but when he is at work in the office, he is very serious and wastes no time.

I understand from others that the things I have said about him also prevail at Acme University, where he is currently an undergraduate.

Without hesitation, I say, give the graduate fellowship to Mr. Brown.

Donald L. Smith

Editor, *Exponent News*

Figure 5.8: Sample of Strong Recommendation Letter
This powerful recommendation mentions all ten qualities noted in the request.

also be used as a marketing tool for consulting and free-lance work.

In my job search workshops, the following questions are often asked regarding creative marketing materials.

> ### SUCCESS ENHANCER
>
> Be on the lookout for opportunities to expand your list of professional accomplishments. Being able to include on your résumé that you gave a speech or a workshop or wrote an article for a professional association not only establishes your technical and professional credibility, but it also speaks volumes about your level of commitment. One presentation per year should suffice, since more than this can detract from your commitment to your job.
>
> Joining a professional organization is an excellent way to gain valuable experience, make solid connections, and expand your accomplishments. A workshop or article done gratis for the association can give you exposure that can lead to lucrative consulting work and job offers as you build your career options.

Can you give me some ideas for putting together a background summary?

Your background summary can be anywhere from one paragraph to one page in length. Anything longer than that would be self-defeating in its complexity. It's important to remember that the purpose of your background summary is to provide sharply focused highlights of your qualifications. It should be clear and simple.

There are a number of ways to achieve this. In my job search workshops, I ask my students to review the literature in their field (trade magazines and journals, professional association bulletins, and training brochures are good sources). These publications feature experts in the field who are writing articles or giving presentations, and a background summary of the recognized expert is usually included. You can use this as a model for preparing your own background summary. Try comparing several samples and build your background summary from a composite of ideas. It's a good idea to save the samples in your Job Search Notebook so that you can easily refer to them and use them to edit and update your own background summary. That way you'll be able to develop a customized marketing tool tailored specifically for your situation.

Do you have any tips for developing a crisp, professional style, oriented toward my field? As a recent grad, I'm afraid my writing style sounds more academic (from a term paper) than businesslike?

Business writing is different from academic writing. And a sharp, professional style tailored to your field is a definite asset for any job seeker. One creative way to achieve this style is to imitate a model

---

123 Fern Lane
Anywhere, USA 12345

May 20, 19__

John Smith
123 Oak Tree Lane
Anywhere, USA 12345

To Whom It May Concern:

sounds unstable — I have worked with John Smith on and off for the past four years, as a Senior Lead Engineer.

a left handed compliment — His knowledge and initiative have been remarkable for his age and I have enjoyed working with him.

could be negative — He has an amazing grasp of things in the realm of electrical engineering, computer programming and engineering writing. John knows his strengths and limitations and is able to clearly analyze conditions and apply persuasion effectively to obtain the confidence of senior engineers and management.

For these reasons, I am happy to recommend John for any position he may seek.

Jim Jones
Standards Engineer

Figure 5.9: Sample of Weak Recommendation Letter John's request letter simply asked for a letter of recommendation with no further detail; this is the disastrous result.

Susan Miller

With degrees in psychology and communications and 15 years' experience in management and communication, Ms. Miller brings a wealth of knowledge and experience to her clients. As Manager of Professional Development at ABC International for ten years, she's gained extensive management expertise. Her main focus is increasing performance and profits through improved communication, customer service, and professional management.

In 1971, Ms. Miller won the prestigious Rotary International Fellowship for graduate study of the University of Acme, where she earned her Masters Degree in Communication and addressed over 50 professional organizations. Since then, she's directed management and development programs for major corporations, universities, government and non-profit organizations. Ms. Miller lectures in graduate management programs at the University of Acme and ABC University. She also appears on nationally syndicated radio programs discussing management and productivity issues. Ms. Miller is listed in <u>Who's Who in Women Executives</u> and <u>Who's Who of American Women</u>.

Since 1978, she has been a successful management/communications consultant. Among her clients are:

Monshanto	YWBA
AT&B	Senior Achievement
Farco	City of Angel
DuFont	Bank of United States
IBN	Ace Electric
Fisney Productions	ABC University

> Ms. Miller's seminars include Effective Work Relationships, Image Skills, Memory Improvement, Business Communication, Technical Writing for Scientists and Engineers, Dynamic Oral Presentations, Motivating Employees, Time Management, Stress Skills, Reading Efficiency, Assertiveness Training, Creative Thinking, Women in Business, Résumés and Interviews, Dual-Career Couples, Effective Meetings, Interaction Management, Group Dynamics, Team Building, Conflict Resolution, Performance Appraisals, Improving Customer Service, leadership and Strategic Thinking, Performance and Productivity Improvement.
>
> Ms. Miller publishes a monthly column in the *West Coast Journal of Business and Management*. She is the author of *Managing Transitions in Business and Life*.

Figure 5.10: Sample Background Summary

from a professional publication. This is particularly helpful for job seekers with limited experience such as recent grads, career changers and re-entry women. Roger used this technique effectively when switching from sales to a research marketing position with a large corporation. He got the business school program catalog and used their current jargon, lingo, and priorities in his cover letter, résumé, and background summary. The courses on marketing in the catalog listed such topics as targeting, segmenting markets, positioning, planning, social marketing, networking, sales dialogue, and direct response. These are powerful terms in the business, which Roger emphasized effectively in his résumé, cover letter, and background summary.

Are there any other creative marketing materials I can use besides recommendations and a background summary?

A portfolio of selected work samples is another creative self-marketing tool. This is common in such professions as art, theater, publishing, modeling, and advertising. But it can also be used successfully by many others. Here are some effective examples that a recruiter for a large conglomerate industry shared with me.

>data processing professional (sample of typing)

>training coordinator (course design and evaluations)

>marketing specialist (marketing plan)

>architect (scale model)

>urban planner (design)

Be creative and put together a few samples of your best work. You can mention this in your first interview and bring your portfolio to the second interview where it will distinguish you from the other candidates.

If you plan to do free-lance work or consulting, a brochure or folder describing your products and services works nicely as a marketing tool. In it you should include several sections:

>your background and qualifications

>your organization (who works with you)

>your products

>your services

>a list of previous clients

>your address, phone and fax numbers

>professional license number (if appropriate)

Make sure you use a creative design. This will present you most favorably and market your services effectively.

As you complete this chapter on Beyond the Basics: Other Marketing Materials, you will have filed the following items in your **Job Search Notebook** under section 5.

>List of Those Familiar With Your Abilities

>Personal Characteristics Desirable to Employers

>Your Outline for Recommendation Request

>Sample Background Summaries

Part Three

Go Out and Get the Job!

CHAPTER 6

Beginning Your Job Search

"A Journey of a thousand miles begins with the first step."

—*Ancient Proverb*

It's been said that failing to plan is planning to fail. So, as you begin your job search, your first step should be to develop a plan. Once you decide how much time you want to give yourself, you can develop a step-by-step time line.

SCHEDULING YOUR JOB SEARCH

Experts recommend that you should allow at least six months for your job search. Research suggests that the old aphorism "haste makes waste" applies here. Going through a careful and thorough analysis to match your needs with those of prospective employers takes some quality time. Finding just any job to pay the bills might take less time, but finding the job that's right for you requires a time-consuming, methodical approach. You can't rush through it. That's why it's important to plan for at least a six-month search, and it's a good idea to develop a schedule (Figure 6.1) for yourself at the beginning of your job search. It is essential that you establish a time frame and pace yourself to a schedule. You should allow a realistic time frame for each step. Keep the schedule in your Job Search Notebook under section 6 and refer to it often.

This approach is, of course, ideal for those with time and living expenses for six months. But if you're suddenly unemployed, with little or no savings, this chapter will give you some ideas on quick ways to contact employers and how to take advantage of the ones with a speedier hiring process. Additionally, Chapter 2 discusses various ways to learn about employers, such as employment agencies and recruiters, which can often lead to immediate employment.

Your plan will keep you moving ahead. It's important to stay motivated by taking at least one action per day. When you get discouraged, taking any action, even one as simple as looking up a phone number, will generate more action and build motivation. When you get stumped, go back to your Job Search Schedule and ask yourself what small action you can take right now to move closer to the next step.

Figure 6.1 provides a sample six-month schedule. You can use the steps outlined here as a model for developing your own, based on your particular time frame. I think it's helpful to have each step outlined at the beginning so you know what to anticipate, how much is involved, and approximately how much time to allow. A schedule motivates you to stay on track with the goals you established in Chapter 1.

It's important to remember that your schedule is only a guide. You're in control, and if one step takes longer than expected, that's O.K. Don't get discouraged. As long as you're moving in the direction of your goals, you will be successful. Because you'll be working on some tasks concurrently, many steps will necessarily overlap, and this may help to speed up the process.

Contacting Employers

Once you've done your initial planning and research, your next task will be to find the best way of contacting employers. What will be most effective: a phone call, a letter, or walk-in? To maximize your chances of success, I recommend using all of these techniques in concert. Each approach will be appropriate at different times and has certain advantages and disadvantages as described in the following paragraphs.

Phone Calls

Believe it or not, a mass phone campaign—calling companies listed in your area can get results. The yellow pages are an excellent place to find a list of employers. I used this method (out of desperation) to get a high school teaching job back in the 70's when there were hundreds of qualified baby-boomers knocking on the door for every position. The key is to be very specific about what you want. Explain this to the person who answers the phone, then ask to speak to the person in charge of hiring for that position. If you think you're being screened, try this approach...Tell the person who answers that you're writing a note to the head of _____ department and need that person's correct title and spelling of their name. Later, you can call back and say, "This is _____ and I'd like to speak with _____ regarding a personal matter. Usually, they'll put you right through with this kind of confident opener. If the person is not there, try calling back during off-hours (early, late, or during lunch) when the secretary probably isn't there and your employer is likely to answer his or her own phone. Once you get them on the line you have an opportunity to sell yourself. Just explain what you have to offer, what you can do for the company and what makes you better than other candidates.

I was looking for a job teaching English, so I called every private

SAMPLE JOB SEARCH SCHEDULE		
A Guide to Success		
Action	Started On Week #	Completed On Week #
1. Set Goals	1 ☐	2 ☐
2. Target Employers	2 ☐	4 ☐
3. Request Recommendations	6 ☐	8 ☐
4. Write Draft Cover Letters	6 ☐	8 ☐
5. Tailor Qualifications	8 ☐	10 ☐
6. Develop Résumés and Final Cover Letters	8–10 ☐	10–12 ☐
7. Contact Employers	12 ☐	14 ☐
8. Schedule Interviews	12–14 ☐	14–16 ☐
9. Rehearse Interviews	12–16 ☐	16–18 ☐
10. Interview Employers	12–18 ☐	18–22 ☐
11. Design Post-Interview Strategy	12–22 ☐	23 ☐
12. Write Acceptance Letter	24 ☐	24 ☐

Figure 6.1

high school in the phone book. I was shocked when I found one that had an opening not only for a teacher, but for a department chairperson. As it turned out, the chairperson had resigned that day, and the job was perfectly suited to my qualifications.

Advantages – This approach works better with small companies who don't need to send all applicants through an impersonal staffing group. It can give you the advantage of getting there before the position is advertised (as my case illustrates). If you're perfect for the job, the company saves advertising and recruiting costs. So it's a mutual win/win.

Disadvantages – This rather unorthodox method can be quite discouraging. It's a real challenge to get through screening receptionists who are trained to screen out unknown callers. But, it can be done! As you make numerous calls, your confident openers and self presentation skills will improve.

Classifieds

Another good way to contact potential employers is through the classified ads. Every daily newspaper has a classified section which lists current job openings and how to contact employers by phone or mail.

Carol, a recent economics grad, used this method to find her first job as a sales assistant at a major stock brokerage firm just outside of New York City. She responded to the classified ad by sending in her résumé and was hired within a week. The problem she found was that the job was not at all what the ad claimed. (Similar to the experience I had with my first job.) But Carol was smarter than I was. She quit after the first week and moved to the Big Apple (more on that job search later).

Advantages – Of course, there are some excellent positions advertised in the classifieds and this is a good way to find a job when you need to start working right away. Business publications such as *The Wall Street Journal, National Business Weekly*, and some trade magazines carry ads nationally for highly desirable positions.

Disadvantages – Fewer than 10 percent of all job openings are advertised. Those that are advertised will usually attract a lot of competition. Because of the high cost of placing the ad, job descriptions are often vague, and because employers want to attract as many prospects as possible, the ad sometimes seems to make the job sound better than it really is (as Carol's case illustrates).

Mail Campaign

Getting mailing lists from professional associations and blanketing the industry with your application package is an effective strategy. Often, you'll get results which will allow you to pick and choose among the lot for the one that meets your specifications. Steve got his first University teaching job in psychology using this strategy. He sent out 100 résumés the same week that the *L.A. Times* ran an article on the scarcity of teaching jobs in the humanities. He felt pretty special when he read that there were at least 100 applicants for some openings in his field and he'd landed a plum position using persistence and creativity.

Even when times are tough and jobs in your field are scarce, there are some jobs out there. The trick is to find them. Some people call this "luck" or "being in the right place at the right time." By increasing the number of applications you make, you're statistically improving your chances of being in the right place at the right time. The law of averages will be on your side. If you send out more résumés than the other candidates, it stands to reason that you'll have a better chance of succeeding than they do. To effectively use this method you'll need to compile a mailing list to include correct spelling of names, titles, company names, and addresses. It's a good idea to call and verify this information. I've known employers to return résumés that were incorrectly addressed with a negative note on accuracy. Once your list is letter perfect you can use the mailing list to address envelopes or prepare labels. Proofread the addresses and then file your mailing list in your Job Search Notebook under section 6.

Advantages – Direct mail maximizes your options by allowing you to survey the industry in your area. A good response can boost your confidence and help you set higher goals. Since 90 percent of open positions are not advertised, a direct mail campaign is a good way to zero in on an upcoming position before the competition hears about it. You also have the added advantage of being able to strategize and send in a lot of extra background material (see Chapter 5 for ideas on this) along with your résumé to impress them. If you do this, you'll stand out because the hiring manager will be reviewing only your application materials. You won't be just another one of thousands who responded to an ad.

Disadvantages – This method can require a lot of time and effort, especially if you're tailoring your résumé and cover letter for particular positions. Addressing a lot of envelopes (I once did 100 on a manual typewriter) can be a painstaking effort, so allow plenty of extra time.

Walk-in

This strategy takes advantage of the fact that fewer than 10 percent of all open positions are advertised. Carol got an excellent job during tough times using the walk-in strategy. When Carol left the brokerage business for life in the Big Apple, she found a job as a junior advertising rep for a small publishing firm on her first day in the city as a walk-in. If you need a job right away and aren't afraid to take risks, pounding the pavement could work for you.

Advantages – This is a strategy that works well because you're leaving yourself open to the possibility of being in the right place at the right time. You have the advantages of self-presentation, which can be very powerful. You can use appearance, personality, style, and gestures influentially. Many managers are impulsive and make decisions on "gut feeling." If they like you—you're hired!

Disadvantages – It can be exhausting and slow because of logistics which make if difficult to cover much ground in one day. And, at many companies you might not get to see the person responsible for hiring. It's not unusual to be asked to just leave your résumé or fill out an application. If you do get to see the hiring manager, you may be catching him or her at a bad time. Often, walk-ins are more effective in small companies where a less structured hiring process allows you to talk with managers and avoid going through the personnel department.

FOLLOW-UP

If you've been following my suggestions, you've contacted many employers, possibly sent out 100 résumés, and made numerous phone calls and walk-in visits. Having made so many contacts, it quickly becomes apparent that you'll need a good way to keep track of them and to easily follow-up on the hopefuls and quickly discard the impossibles. This is important in tough times when it may be necessary to make seemingly endless contacts.

A system like the Contact/Response Chart (Figure 6.2) works well. Make as many copies of the form as you think you'll need to track your contacts. Record the information on each employer and then file the completed form in your Job Search Notebook under section 6 for future reference at the interview stage.

If you haven't received a response to your initial contact within ten business days, you may want to follow up with a different contact technique. Managers appreciate follow-up calls on the résumé you sent in or the walk-in visit. This shows that you're still interested. Sometimes, particularly in large organizations in tough times, the hiring process can be lengthy and cumbersome (requiring several levels of approval and other staffing considerations).

During this process, if a manager really wants you, he or she may be concerned that you've lost interest. So, it's a good idea to let them know that you're still a candidate. As some of your competition drops out, the follow-up strategy will work in your favor.

Information on how to follow up after the interview will be discussed in Chapter 7.

Are there any creative ways to get an interview?

Simply sending in your application and résumé are not enough. Perhaps you feel there's something in your background that will create an automatic bias. In such cases, you can use a professional association to your advantage. Jason, an industrial security specialist for a medium-size industrial waste firm, used this technique effectively. Since 90 percent of the open positions aren't even advertised, Jason decided that instead of applying for advertised positions, he'd simply contact the officers of his professional association's local chapter. These would most certainly be leaders in the industry and in their companies. During his initial contact, he explained that he was new in town and wanted to chat about the local chapter's professional program. He was cordially invited to their offices for a mentoring chat. Jason had done his homework, so once he had his foot in the door—literally!—he was able to ask intelligent questions, learn about the needs of the company, and position himself to fill those needs. It worked like a charm, and he got an offer from his top choice.

How many times should I call an employer to follow up after I've sent in my résumé?

It's a two-sided coin. If you call too many times, you can be labeled a pest, and this will work against you. If you don't call back often enough, another more aggressive candidate may beat you. Most managers agree that if you really want the job, and you think you have a chance, keep calling about once a week. If the manager doesn't seem interested (some people have trouble saying no), then don't waste your time.

How can I identify and join a professional association?

Your local library or college career center will have this information available. Ask your librarian or counselor for help. The listings they

Employer
Position _____
Company_____
Manager (Name & Title)_____
Secretary _____
Address _____
_____
Phone_____
Date Contacted_____
How did I learn about position?
___blind ad (which publication)
___regular ad (which publication)
___unsolicited
___mutual acquaintance (name)
___professional society (name)
___yellow pages
___other _____
Response Received
Date _____
Phone_____
_____
Letter _____
_____
Second Contact
Date _____
Notes _____
_____
Interview
Who _____
Where_____
Date _____
Time _____
Directions _____
_____
Parking_____
_____
Comments_____
_____

Figure 6.2: Contact/Response Chart

provide should give the address and phone number of the national and regional offices. You can contact them to learn about membership application. Often potential new members will be invited to attend their first meeting as a guest before joining. This will give you an opportunity to mingle and evaluate the organization. If there is more than one chapter or association in your area, it would be worthwhile to do some comparison shopping, since your association can be a critical job search tool.

As you complete this chapter and begin your job search, you will have filed the following items in your **Job Search Notebook.**

Job Search Schedule

Employer Mailing Lists

Contact Response Chart

CHAPTER 7

How to Have a Great Interview

"Self-confidence is the first requisite of achievement."

—*Samuel Johnson*

The interview is your chance to really sell yourself, and, from the employer's perspective, this is the most important part of the selection process. The purpose of the interview is to get the job! Your résumé and cover letter are teasers. They got attention for you and attracted the employer's interest, but the interview will determine whether you're right for the job.

Carefully preparing for the interview is even more critical than résumé preparation. Many people have difficulty preparing for an interview because they don't know what to expect. This leads to anxiety, created by fear of the unknown—and anxiety is not a useful emotion in interview preparation! Instead of worrying about everything that could go wrong, you can prepare yourself for a successful interview by focusing on the positive and developing an action plan.

Controlling nervousness is a critical concern in preparing for an interview. For most of us, it's not easy to control our nervousness in a pressure situation. That's why knowing how to plan, prepare, and rehearse for an interview is so important. In this chapter, you'll find pointers for planning every aspect of your interview, preparing for even the most difficult questions, and rehearsing everything you'll need for a great interview.

WHAT TO EXPECT IN AN INTERVIEW

How do employers respond to tough economic times? Usually by trimming their staffs to the bone. There are therefore likely to be few openings, with many well-qualified contenders for each position.

Employers will be very selective indeed, and they're likely to be evaluating each candidate on more than job skills; they'll also be looking for qualities that will help their businesses in tough times. Traits such as commitment, a willingness to go the extra mile, the ability to work well under pressure, and innovation are especially valued in tough times.

Interview strategy doesn't always go as planned. Some interviewers will want to take control and steer you in their direction. In that case, go with the flow. Anything else could work against you. Remember your goal is to convince your interviewer that you're right for this job. Synchronizing your communication style with that of the interviewer can be a powerful advantage. The tricks are to:

relax

be yourself

show enthusiasm

And, if you've planned and rehearsed your material thoroughly, the rest will take care of itself.

Tips from experienced managers and recruiters will give you special insight into what impresses them most in interviews, as well as into what they *don't* like to see.

Study Your Strengths And Weaknesses

Your goal in the interview is to sell yourself by highlighting your personal and career strengths and dealing effectively with your weaknesses. At previous stages of your job search, you analyzed your abilities to identify the right career, employer, and job. You listed your strengths for your cover letter and résumé. In preparing for the interview, it's a good idea to review this information in your Job Search Notebook under section 7 and compile a new list of the highlights (Figure 7.1) appropriate to the position for which you're interviewing. Your list should include abilities and job skills as well as personal self-management characteristics and your background. Try to include an anecdote or performance example to support personal characteristics. It's not enough to say "I'm really good with people" or "I work well under pressure." I hear these clichés all the time in interviews and they always fall flat because they're meaningless. To avoid this trap, I suggest preparing your **Self-Description Guide** (Figure 7.1). File this in your Job Search Notebook under Section 7 and keep this information at your fingertips for the interview. To be convincing you need to support these statements by describing situations where you were successful with some very difficult people or some extraordinary pressure.

Some interviewers will ask you for this information, and some may not. At any rate, you need to be prepared. And if the interviewer *doesn't* ask, you can volunteer the information. This will definitely work to your advantage.

Once you've identified the strengths you want to highlight and have prepared examples, you're ready to work on your weaknesses. Many interviewers still use the classic question that asks you to identify your main weakness. It's a plus to show that you're aware of your weaknesses and are actively taking steps to compensate for them. I once interviewed an applicant for a business teaching position in a large university who stated that he didn't have any weaknesses. To me, this was a dead giveaway for arrogance, conceit, lack of self-insight and an array of undesirable qualities. Someone who's aware of his or her weaknesses is likely to be a better team player and interested in self-improvement. Employers like this in a candidate, so it's to your advantage to identify a few weaknesses that can be dealt with effectively in the interview.

Don't be too self-deprecating, however, as this could work against you. Stay away from anything that could make you seem incompetent, such as being disorganized or having time-management problems. Instead, focus on weaknesses that are an outgrowth of something positive. For instance, a candidate I interviewed recently for a human resources management position told me that her main weakness is that she has a tendency to take on too much at the office. Of course, an employer could also see this as a strength, particularly when she quickly added examples to show how she curbs this tendency and has it under control. Another weakness that can be dealt with effectively is delegation. Admitting that you should delegate more or follow up more on what you've assigned shows that you're aware of a problem area in your management style and are taking steps to correct it. Few managers are able to see themselves in this light, so it's a good way to turn a weakness into a strength. Don't forget to follow your admission with at least one story of self-correction. File your list of weaknesses and support stories in your Job Search Notebook under the interview section for future reference when you rehearse for your interview.

I can't say it often enough: Being well-prepared and focusing on the positive is the best way to have a successful interview. Don't allow yourself to even *think* about a bad interview. Mark Twain's words "I've suffered a great many catastrophes in my life. Most of them never happened" apply here. It's a self-fulfilling prophesy: if you *think* you're going to do well, you'll project self-confidence, and self-confidence is the key to success in an interview situation.

Self-Description Guide

Technical Skills—Be very specific.
    What are your main strengths?
    What is your specialization?
    What do you enjoy the most?
    New things you want to learn?
    Any unique skill combinations?
    What makes you right for this job?

Your Background—Outline appropriate details.
    education
    job history
    reasons for moving
    Why you want to go into or progress in this field?
    What attracts you to this position?
    What do you have to offer the company?
    How does your background qualify you for this position?

Self-Management—Prepare an anecdote for each.
How are you at:
    problem solving?
    decision making?
    interpersonal skills?
    goal setting?

How do you deal with:
    stress?
    long hours?
    working on a team?
    change?
    failure?
    conflict?

Figure 7.1

Research the Job

If you've been following my suggestions during the job search process, you've already done a thorough analysis of your targeted employers in Chapter 2 (Figure 2.2). It would be helpful to review that analysis now. If you haven't yet done the research, you can use the model provided in Figure 2.3 as a guide.

In addition to researching the company, you also need to learn as much as you can about the job before you interview. Knowing what the company is looking for can give you valuable clues to the kinds of questions you'll be asked. Job descriptions in ads are often sketchy and don't give you much to go on. How can you get the information you need?

- Call the hiring manager or recruiter and ask about the job. Try to get such information as how long the position has been vacant. If it's newly created, there's likely to be a greater emphasis on innovation. Are there any special projects waiting in the wings? Who will interview you? What is this person like?

- Talk to people you've met through networking or referrals from your professional association who work there. Try to get a copy of the department newsletter.

- Talk to people from your professional association who hold similar positions at other companies. What are the demands and rewards of the job? What are the politics of moving ahead in the field?

Record the findings of your research in your Job Search Notebook in section 7, "Research for the Interview," and use it when preparing your presentation and interview rehearsal.

Standing Out From The Competition: Your Interview Strategy

Psychologists and consultants who coach employers on structured or behavioral interviewing believe that past behavior is the best indicator of future performance. In tough times, hiring the most predictably productive employees becomes paramount. Interviewers will thus seek concrete, measurable accomplishments and probe for detail as well as hidden motivations. Even unsophisticated interviewers who resort to the traditional open-ended "Tell me about yourself..." style will be impressed when you're prepared to present the quantifiable, specific details of your achievements that demonstrate the right skills for the job at hand.

In preparing your résumé, you laid the groundwork for this part of your interview. Although you can assume the employer has read your résumé, he or she may not recall your accomplishments at the interview. Don't let this throw you. Simply refer to the résumé and add further detail to enhance your achievements. One very busy manager of a large telecommunications company told me that he didn't have time to even read the résumé before the applicant arrived. He was so impressed by the way the applicant for a secretarial position took control of the interview that he hired her on the spot.

Figure 7.2 provides an **Achievements Presentation Planning Sheet** to help stimulate your thinking and get your ideas organized. You should fill out the planning sheet and file it in the interview section of your Job Search Notebook under section 7 to use during the rehearsal stage.

During the interview you'll want to keep this information figuratively in your hip pocket until you have a good feel for what the interviewer is looking for. You can take control of the interview by very briefly answering the interviewer's initial questions and then transitioning to a two-way interview by expressing an interest in the job and the company with your questions. Managers like this very much. Use the first part of the interview to find out what's expected in the job, what the company's business goals are, and what problems exist.

You need to go into the interview with a flexible strategy. At the beginning, try to keep the focus on your background in general. Help the interviewer become acquainted with where you are in your career, previous jobs, schooling, and your reason for making a move at this time. Then try to steer the interview to focus more on the job at hand. This is your chance to interview the interviewer. Find out why the position is open, how this spot fits in with the rest of the department and other departments, how the company is organized, and what problems they are currently trying to overcome. Then move to your role and find out how you can make a contribution to solving the problems and meeting company goals.

With this information on hand you can tailor the presentation of your achievements (still in your hip pocket) to the job your employer has described. Most people make the mistake of immediately trying to impress the employer with how great they are, how smart they are, and how many wonderful things they've done, when the employer is only interested in what you can do for him or her. Showing how you can directly contribute to department goals is far more impressive than the greatest accomplishments (which may or may not be relevant). I once interviewed a very bright MBA, who had graduated first in his class from a top-notch business school, for a budget analyst position. This applicant did a good job of trying to impress me with his 4.0 GPA, but he didn't express any interest in my department or my company. I ended up hiring another applicant, a young woman with a 3.0 GPA from a small unknown college. The enthusiasm she demonstrated in the interview for solving my department's problems and working toward company goals won her the job.

The key to success is the ability to connect your strengths with the employer's goals. Depending on the interviewer's style, you may want to save some of your presentation for questions later in the interview. Or you can wait for an opportunity to connect your

---

Achievements Presentation Planning Sheet

List your achievements and contributions to department and company goals. If you've followed my advice and detailed quantifiable accomplishments on your résumé, you can lift that information and use it on this sheet to prepare your interview script. Be specific. Quantify everything. For example:

  doubled sales 2 years in a row

  increased enrollment by ___ percent

  implemented $10K annual cost savings by doing ___

  produced 50-page catalog

  designed new ___ system to save ___ hours/dollars

  solved x problem in ___ (record time)

  got system up and running in ___ (record time)

  organized number of people to accomplish ___ in ___ (record time)

List your responsibilities and their value to the department (manage YXZ quality program which ensures product integrity and customer satisfaction. Other strategies include: showing growth and improvement; plans for future contributions.

Figure 7.2

achievements to a matching requirement when it comes up. And, if it doesn't come up, you can always add it by saying, "Let me tell you about..."

How can you determine whether a potential employer and job is right for you? First, ask questions, then watch carefully to see whether a prospective employer's behavior matches its self-proclaimed attributes. Find out if upward mobility means the same thing to you as it does to them. (At my first job, my employer's idea of upward mobility was to allow me to go upstairs and get my boss's coffee instead of making it myself!) It pays to get specific about what you expect and what employers offer. Simply responding to questions from the interviewer can potentially limit the information you're presenting. To maximize your opportunities during the interview you need to allow the interviewer to feel a sense of control while you subtly direct the conversation for you advantage. This requires a great deal of skill—skill that most of your competitors will probably be lacking.

If you've done a good job in targeting the right employer, you'll be able to use some of the information from your research to prepare questions for the interviewer.

Handling The Questions: What—And What Not—To Say

For most people, questions are the core of the interview. They determine your success or failure. Therefore, they create the greatest anxiety and strike at our basic fear of the unknown. The best way to dispel this fear is to become familiar with the type of questions likely to be asked. You can then prepare and rehearse your answers so that you'll feel comfortable with any questions you encounter.

Almost any question you'll be asked will fall into one of these 3 categories:

technical skill

background

self-management

Since you can't know exactly what questions the interviewer will ask, the best way to prepare is to develop descriptions of yourself as you've done with Figure 7.1 in each of these areas. Your descriptions should cover all the main points you want to highlight in each area as well as enough detail to prepare you for probing questions. That way, no matter what comes up, you'll be ready.

When the interviewer asks a question, there are several strategies you can use to compose yourself and organize your thoughts. If it's a lengthy, complex, or tricky question, you can paraphrase for clarification. If the question is ambiguous, you need to quickly focus on the most advantageous angle and go with that. Another technique is to ask the speaker to repeat the question. This will help clarify any ambiguity and give you more time to think. An unintimidating way to ask for a repeat would be to say something like "I'm not sure I understand the question, could you please repeat it?" Using "I" language takes the onus off the speaker and puts the responsibility for not understanding on your shoulders.

Answering a question with a question can sometimes be the best technique. (When reporters asked President John F. Kennedy why Irishmen always answer a question with another question, he replied, "Do they?") This technique can give you power, and it is particularly useful when you suspect that your interviewer is a graduate of the Attila the Hun Charm School! One of my résumé interview workshop participants, a doctor on staff at a major teaching hospital, told me that an interviewer once complained, "I've hired people like you before and they never worked out." He asked, "Why not?" and while the interviewer was busy answering the candidate, he got time to develop a positive strategy.

Silence can be effective and powerful. Don't be afraid to pause for a moment, take a deep breath and smile before answering. Saying something like, "I'm glad you asked that—let's see...where should I begin...?" gives you time to collect your thoughts. Humor can also be an effective tool. If used correctly, without malice or arrogance, it can ease tension, help you relax, and give both parties a chance to see each other's human side. Be careful, though – if used incorrectly (to hurt someone), humor can come across as arrogant or flippant. Self-deprecating humor is the safest.

As many companies are downsizing in these tough economic times, hiring the right person with a high productivity potential becomes critical to employers. For this reason, many managers seem to be adopting an adversarial interview style. And job seekers in these tough times are increasingly intimidated and concerned over how to handle difficult interviewers. Questions that could only be designed to shock or insult (let's see how he handles stress) are difficult for even the most self-confident applicant. How can we prepare ourselves to deal with this kind of pressure?

There are several simple, yet very effective techniques that work well in these intimidating situations. The techniques can be rehearsed with a partner before the interview so that you'll be able to deal confidently with any situation.

Probing questions, designed to see how well you deal with stress and hold up under pressure, are one strategy used as part of their interview assessment.

Tough economic times have a way of making employers get tough in interviews. If you're not prepared for it, the tough interview format (sometimes called behavioral or structural interviewing) can come as a shock. One recent marine biology grad in my interview workshop was so humiliated by her interviewer that she lost her cool and walked out. Later she regretted the fact that she'd eliminated herself from the running. But there *are* ways to prepare for the tough interview and use it to your advantage. Doing just a little more research and preparation will put you miles ahead of your competition.

If you've done a good job preparing your self-descriptions (Figure 7.1) you'll have focused information at your fingertips for dealing with even the most difficult issues. Here are some sample tough questions and strong answers.

Samples of Tricky Questions

INTERVIEWER: Why aren't you earning more? or Why weren't you promoted more quickly?

STRATEGY: *Focus on skill development.*

APPLICANT: "I chose to stay with that small company, even though the pay was lower, because they gave me opportunities to learn by doing a number of different tasks such as...(describe tasks and skills learned)."

INTERVIEWER: Why have you moved around so much?

STRATEGY: *Emphasize the positive.*

APPLICANT: "A number of factors made each move attractive for me:

    upward mobility

    logistics (closer to home, etc.)

    broader experience opportunity"

    (Give details on each.)

INTERVIEWER: Sell me on yourself or on our product.

STRATEGY: *Do you homework and rehearse diligently.*

APPLICANT: If you've done your homework on your Self-

Description Guide (Figure 7.1) and Achievements Presentation Planning Sheet (Figure 7.2) you'll have all the information you need in your hip pocket. And if you've thoroughly researched the company using the Employer Profile Worksheet (Figures 2.7 and 2.8) you'll be knowledgeable enough to do an excellent sales presentation.

INTERVIEWER: Tell me about your best boss or job and your worst boss or job.

STRATEGY: *Focus on the positive. Turn weaknesses to strengths. Your challenge is to create realistic scenarios that will highlight your strengths. Avoid any sour grapes.*

APPLICANT: One successful candidate, an entertainment executive interviewed recently for a program director position, answered it this way:

"My worst boss was a manager who didn't delegate well. He had a tendency to drop the ball and run. I soon learned how to go back and ask the right questions to get the information I needed to get the job done. I learned to draw up preliminary plans or work through part one and then check to see if I was headed in the right direction. After a while this system worked very well and I gained a great deal of skill learning to manage my boss's weakness.

"My best boss was the one who gave me a lot of responsibility and latitude. I made my own decisions and was accountable for the results, reporting routinely to the boss."

INTERVIEWER: What would you do if…two staff members began verbally attacking each other in a meeting; your department was understaffed and a major project was behind schedule; your boss asked you to do something unethical?

STRATEGY: *Such a question is designed to test your reactions under pressure. The pressure of the interview simulates job pressure to perform in such areas as: problem-solving, decision-making, conflict-resolution and interpersonal skills, and your ability to deal with your emotions. It can be tricky and complicated.*

APPLICANT: Start by getting clarification to make sure you understand the question. This can be done by paraphrasing. This will also buy you a little extra time to collect your thoughts. If you've done your homework well, you'll have already identified both hypothetical and real situations that highlight your strengths (support stories from Figure 7.1 and your list of weaknesses filed in your Job Search Notebook under section 7.) Mentally scan your selections and choose one that's closely related to the interviewer's scenario. You can always buy time by prefacing your story with something like "I'm glad you asked about that, because something just like that situation happened to me recently at...." Then tell your story, focusing on two or three critical skills you want to highlight. Summarize by itemizing what you learned from the experience.

INTERVIEWER: How do you deal with conflict?

STRATEGY: *Focus on a simple process that can be applied effectively in many different situations. Give examples.* A manager at a small legal services firm shared this response she received from a recent secretarial applicant with me, which she thought was an excellent response—concise and to the point.

APPLICANT: "Any time people work together over a period of time, some conflict is inevitable, so I take it in stride. First, I look for areas of agreement that we can build on. Then I find out what the other person wants and explore ways to create a win/win situation."

INTERVIEWER: Why do you want this job?

STRATEGY: *Re-emphasize the contributions you want to make to this company and how well-qualified you are to make those contributions. Highlight your most prominent accomplishments and talents.*

APPLICANT: "I'm convinced that my background and skills make me the right person for the job." Then go on to give specific examples by relating the requirements of this job to your previous experience.

INTERVIEWER: Is there anything else I need to know about you?

STRATEGY: *Use this as a final opportunity to sell yourself. Always save some small points that may not be central to the job but that could be a real plus in tough times, for this stage of the interview.* If the question doesn't come up, you can always bring it up yourself.

APPLICANT: "Yes, I thought you might like to know that at XYZ I also did some design and layout work which, combined with my other experience, would allow me to effectively pinch-hit for several functions."

INTERVIEWER: What salary are you looking for?

STRATEGY: *Keep your thoughts as close to the vest as possible. Save this discussion for the second interview if you can.*

APPLICANT: "Could we discuss salary later? I'd like to spend today learning more about the position." If the interviewer persists, get him or her to make the first move by asking, "What's the salary range for this position?" If you've done your homework, you'll have a good feel for what to expect. If the interviewer insists on discussing salary, you'll have a prepared response. If you're forced to give a number, use a range keeping the low side around 20 percent higher than your current salary. Think of this as a starting point for your negotiation, which will probably be conducted later. During the interview it's important to keep the focus on the job and your qualifications. Emphasize that it's the job that's important to you, and that salary is a secondary issue which will be discussed after they make you an offer.

INTERVIEWER: Do you have any questions?

STRATEGY: *This is your chance to showcase your research findings and position yourself as a strong candidate. Ask informal questions about industry trends, company products and results. Show an interest in division, corporate, and department goals. Dave, an office equipment sales rep, shared his successful response with me. It won him the job in spite of tough competition.*

APPLICANT: "It's remarkable how Widgets Incorporated has maintained increased earnings for the last ten years—even with the tough competition and industry downturn. What are you doing at this division to deal so effectively with the changing environment?" This type of question demonstrates your enthusiasm for the company and shows that you've done your homework. It also will work to your advantage because it allows the manager to talk about one of his or her favorite subjects and provides you with valuable information.

INTERVIEWER: Where do you see yourself in five years?

STRATEGY: *This could be a trick question to see whether you want the interviewer's job or whether you're trying to move up too fast. On the other hand, if you don't show any aspirations, you could appear to be lacking motivation. The best strategy is to tailor your answer to what you know about the department. If you've done your research thoroughly, you'll know what the next step up in that department should be and you can zero in on that. If you've learned that this department doesn't have such a career ladder, you can always focus on growth with something like:*

APPLICANT: "When I think back on the last five years and see how much I've grown and how much experience has taught me, I look forward to learning as much in the next five years." Keeping the emphasis on personal growth, you might try comparing yourself to a role model or mentor (such as a previous boss) and describing how you'd like to be as skilled as they are in a particular area. Answer questions concisely. Being brief will help you stay focused and get your points across. Interviewers will appreciate your ability to deal with the issues effectively and to stay on track. This will also score points for you as a career skill.

What Not to Say (Solicited and Unsolicited)

It's a mistake to bring up:

1) anything personal

2) anything negative about yourself or your previous employment situations

Always focus on the positive. If a question is asked regarding how you deal with problems or weaknesses, you should immediately turn this into a positive as we discussed earlier in this chapter.

Never bring up anything about your family, friends, life-style, or other personal issues. Keep the focus of the interview on job-related topics. It is illegal for employers to ask about such issues, and you should avoid bringing them up. If you're asked an illegal question, simply respond by bringing it back to job issues, saying something like: "Is this a requirement of the job?"

Body Language and Other Nonverbal Communication

Because self-confident success is exactly what you want to project in the interview, your body language must remain consistent with this message. Everything about you must support and reinforce your confidence. Your voice, demeanor, gestures, and facial expression can add to or detract from your credibility.

One of the most interesting psychological discoveries of the twentieth century is that action precedes feeling. In other words, if we *act* self-confident we'll soon begin to *feel* self-confident. If you force yourself to stand and sit with rib cage high, shoulders back and head erect, you'll feel self-assured and you'll project confidence. If you relax your facial muscles and smile, you'll feel positive and relaxed. If you keep your hands and feet still while seated, you'll feel calm inside.

Demeanor – Employers are looking for an energetic and enthusiastic attitude, and the way you enter a room makes a strong statement about your attitude. Practice an even, energetic stride—not too fast, since that can make you look nervous, or too slow, which may make you appear lazy!

Carriage and Posture – The way you sit and stand says a lot about your self-confidence and feeling of power. Hold your head erect, and your rib cage high (this will naturally push your shoulders back and your stomach in). Concentrating on self-confident carriage will also help you to overcome nervousness. Check your carriage on your video tape.

Dancers know that the pelvis is the seat of power. Taking your cue from them, make sure that your pelvis is centered on the chair. Resist the nervous temptation to sit on the edge of your seat. Centering your pelvis will help you feel more relaxed and confident.

Eye Contact – Your eyes are, it is said, the mirror of your soul, the window to your mind. Make-up, hair-style, clothing, jewelry, and accessories should be orchestrated to draw the listener's attention to your eyes—not to those items themselves. You want your eyes to reflect sincerity and credibility. It's important to maintain appropriate eye contact during the interview. How much eye contact is appropriate? Sometimes, it's difficult to know for sure. Too much eye contact can be intimidating, while not enough eye contact breeds mistrust. Take your cue from the other person: see what level of eye contact the interviewer seems to go for, and follow suit.

Gestures – The way you use your hands can enhance or detract from your message. Gestures are important because they project energy and enthusiasm. Without them, your presentation will seem flat and lifeless. On the other hand, if your gestures are too dramatic or fidgety, the listener's attention will be on the gestures instead of on your message. Be natural, and make sure your gestures enhance and illustrate your point instead of being distracting. Don't cross your arms.

Facial Expression – When you're tense or nervous, your facial expression can give you away. This could work against you in an interview. Pay attention to facial expression during your rehearsal. You want to project a professional image that is confident and serious, yet at the same time relaxed and friendly. The best way to develop this is with practice. Use the mirror and video camera until it all comes naturally and you feel very confident.

Habits – When faced with a stressful situation, we all experience nervous reactions such as fidgeting, nail biting, or butterflies in the stomach. To help overcome these tendencies there are a few things you can do in the reception area just before the interview. Try deep breathing and muscle relaxation exercises. Studies have shown that increased oxygen in your bloodstream relaxes muscles and enhances performance. Use mind tricks. Pretend that you're an actor playing the role of the most perfect candidate for the job. Or, pretend that the interviewer is your closest friend.

Tilting the head – This is a coy expression, one used more often by women—and it will definitely work against you by undermining your credibility. If you have a tendency to tilt your head to one side, take note of this in your role playing and make a special effort to keep your head held high. This will also enhance your self-confidence.

Tone of Voice – Studies have shown that tone of voice is more powerful than language in conveying your message. If your voice sounds tired, angry, hostile, or unsure, you detract considerably from your image of professional power and self-confidence. When faced with a stressful situation, many women have a tendency to unintentionally speak in shrill tones. For this reason, it's a good idea for women to try to lower their voices when under stress. Pay special attention to projecting energy and enthusiasm in your voice.

Clarity of Speech – Many people tend to stutter, mispronounce words, or slur their words together when under pressure. Practice articulation when you rehearse the interview. Then, right before the interview, try the following exercises in the reception area (or maybe in the car or restroom, for privacy!): to relax your voice, lips, and tongue, take several deep breaths, exhale through your mouth, yawn, and repeat a silly tongue twister. This will get you laughing at yourself and make you relax even more.

Language – Choice of vocabulary is important. Using slang or vulgar words will quickly discredit you. Use a professional, business-like vocabulary and a natural, conversational style. Trying to impress the interviewer with sophisticated language and buzzwords will only make you sound phony.

Rate of Speech – Talking too fast is a common sign of nervousness. Watch out for the runaway motor mouth, which can turn on automatically and get you into trouble! If you've carefully planned and rehearsed what you want to say, this shouldn't happen. But if you know you have this tendency, you'll need to make a conscious effort to slow down.

Humor – After your careful scripting and diligent rehearsals, you may be feeling like a programmed robot. Yet the key to success is remaining flexible and relaxed. Remember, if you've done your homework and prepared yourself well, you'll be confident of your role and you can be yourself. Show your human side. Let your personality shine through. A little wit and humor can go a long way.

Nervous Laughter – Nervous laughter is a bad habit you should guard against. Women in particular may sometimes have a tendency to giggle under pressure. In some situations this can be effective in diffusing tension, but in an interview it will quickly destroy your credibility.

Energy – Energy is one of the primary qualifiers, particularly in tough economic times. Employers need energetic go-getters in their organizations who can go out there and solve problems, capture new accounts, and come up with innovative ideas. *This is the characteristic that will distinguish you from your competition when all else is equal.* How do you project energy in an interview? Make everything about your presentation crisp and forceful. Every detail on your checklist, from your erect carriage, energetic stride, and confident voice to your natural gestures will project energy.

Enthusiasm – Managers and personnel directors consistently rate enthusiasm as a winning trait. How can you show enthusiasm in the interview? Do your homework—learning all you can about the company, the position, and the company's products or services clearly demonstrates your enthusiasm. Displaying an interest in making a contribution to department and company goals shows impressive enthusiasm. This is an easy way to score points over your competition and really shine in the interview.

Listening – In the interview, as in business and life, listening is a critical skill. In his research into listening, the eminent psychologist Ralph Nichols found that 60 percent of all mistakes at work are caused by poor listening. Because the natural human tendency is to mentally prepare one's own response while the other person is speaking, we must constantly guard against this tendency and work at listening. Here's a simple formula for better listening that a seminar leader, Sam Horn, shared with me.

L ook and lean (maintain eye contact and lean toward speaker)
I gnore distractions
S uspend judgement
T ell them what you heard (paraphrase)
E xperience their side (empathize)
N o interrupting

Paraphrasing, the fourth item on the list, is an especially effective technique because it allows you to clarify any misunderstandings and gives the speaker a chance to hear his or her ideas played back (which is always an ego-boost!). An additional benefit of paraphrasing is that it gives you some time to think about what your response will be.

"So you're saying…," "Let's see if I understand this…," and "You're saying…," are good ways to begin paraphrasing. If it's relatively simple, you can simply repeat the other person's words:

INTERVIEWER: "Tell me about your weaknesses."
APPLICANT: "Let's see, what are my weaknesses?"

Nonverbal Communication: Clothing and Accessories

Studies have found that up to 90 percent of our messages are communicated nonverbally. To project power and self-confidence in the interview, your appearance and nonverbal cues must be as polished and consistent as your professional message.

This section details industry-specific guidelines for appropriate appearance, including budget considerations, color and cut of clothing, hairstyle, accessories, and even eyeglasses. Failure to recognize that there are subtle expectations for different industries and for different positions within any industry can work against you. Being aware of these expectations and knowing how to project the appropriate image are key skills. Knowing that you look your best and that you're dressed just right for your interview will also enhance your self-esteem enormously.

For both men and women, I advise against wearing fragrance of any kind. The interviewer may be allergic to it or he or she may feel overwhelmed by it or have an aversion to the particular fragrance.

At your interview, you should dress appropriately for your industry. In industries other than fashion, art, and entertainment, the watchword is conservative. And if you're not sure about your industry, it's better to err on the conservative side. If you're in the fashion, art, or entertainment industry, you'll have more latitude. But even within these industries, expectations vary widely, so it's a good idea to research the company where you're interviewing.

Color and Cut of Clothing – Studies have shown that the most successful colors in interviews are neutral shades—for example, off white, light blue, grey, and tan. Solid colors work best. Stay away from bold plaids or prints, which can look too sporty. Because people react psychologically to color, your choice makes an important statement. The neutral colors suggested here are friendly and persuasive. Bright colors such as red or yellow can be intimidating. Strong colors such as black and white can be too harsh for persuasion. Women should avoid wearing pink or peach in business situations because they can detract from your credibility. If you feel you need to add some color, you can add interest to your outfit with a colorful scarf or pocket kerchief.

The cut of your clothing should be tailored and conservative. Men should always wear a jacket and tie; women should wear a business suit or tailored dress and jacket. Skirts should be a conservative length (nothing above the knee).

Hairstyle – Again, conservative and tailored are the watchwords. No

Bart Simpson style for men or Godiva length for women! If you have long hair, it should be pulled back or up for the interview. Your hairstyle should frame your face because this is where you want to focus your interviewer's attention. Therefore, you don't want anything about your hairstyle to distract attention from you and your ideas.

Jewelry – This should be carefully planned to support and enhance your professional image. Watches, for example, should be conservative to project a serious, professional image rather than brightly colored plastic, which suggests fun and frivolity. Jewelry should be kept simple to focus attention on you. Too much jewelry or elaborately styled jewelry draws attention to itself and will work against you in the interview. Too much jewelry is a turn-off, and many managers have told me they won't hire someone who looks like a Christmas tree because it's bad for the company image, particularly in service-oriented businesses.

Shoes and Stockings – For women, conservative closed-toed pumps in a shade that matches your hemline are recommended. If your shoes don't match your hemline, they should be a lighter shade—never darker. Men should wear dark dress shoes or loafers—no boots or patent leather or athletic type shoes. Men's socks should match or coordinate with trouser color and should be long enough so that no leg shows when you sit down.

Women should always wear stockings. In one of my interview workshops, a recruiter for a large automobile corporation once told me that she knows managers who will not hire a woman who shows up at an interview without stockings. To some people, bare legs in a business setting indicate sloppiness and lack of attention to detail.

Your stockings should complement the rest of your outfit and enhance your overall professional image. My favorite choice for a really together, finished look is to select stockings and shoes the same shade as your hemline. This look works well for all figure types. Neutral shades and light colors—that is, lighter than the hemline—also work well if you have slim legs. Black and navy should only be worn with matching hemlines and shoes.

Definitely stay away from patterned or sequined hose, and from seamed hose as well (these are a bit too sexy for an interview). It's better to save these styles for evening!

Briefcase/Handbag – For both men and women, I recommend leaving the briefcase at home. It's unnecessary and will be just one more thing to worry about: where to put it, or having to dig through it and appearing disorganized. It's much better and sleeker looking to carry only a portfolio. This is perfect for keeping copies of your résumé, recommendations, and extra paper for taking notes. For women, it's better not to carry a handbag, but if you must, choose a small, tailored bag the same color as your shoes.

Glasses – Surveys of interviewers have found that applicants who wear glasses are perceived as more intelligent, serious, and knowledgeable. Their earning power is also estimated at a much higher level. So, on interview day, it pays to put your contact lenses away. And just for fun, to see if the studies are right, if you don't wear corrective lenses, you can purchase flattering frames with clear glass.

In making your selection, go for the serious look. Pastel or brightly colored frames with jeweled corners project an image of fun and frivolity, and so should be avoided. Also avoid glasses with colored lenses, which make it difficult to see your eyes and are distracting to the interviewer. For your interview you want the serious, intelligent look.

For Women Only

Makeup – The purpose of makeup is to enhance your natural features. Daytime makeup for business should always be kept simple. It's important to make sure that you've selected the right shades for your clothing and skin tones. If you're not sure about this, many department stores and cosmetic retailers have consultants who will be happy to advise you. This seemingly minor improvement can make a big difference in the way you are perceived.

Nail Polish – Unless you're in the fashion or art industry, your nails should be short to medium length, with clear or neutral polish. Anything more than this can be distracting. A manager who works for a major city newspaper told me that her manager will not promote or hire women who come to the interview with long, brightly colored nails.

Rehearsing for the Interview

Once you've prepared your presentation and practiced your replies to tricky questions, it's simply a matter of studying your part and rehearsing your lines for the final performance. The best way to do this is to record the information filed in section 7 of your Job Search Notebook in the days or weeks before your interview. Use every spare moment to read and rehearse your lines. By the time of your interview those ideas will be so imbedded in your mind that you'll be in full command of your responses.

Also, use your time before the interview to visualize yourself successfully completing the interview. Picture every detail vividly, from your clothing and hairstyle to your calm composure and confident posture. Imagine yourself answering every tough question with poise. See yourself enjoying the conversation, smiling and using humor appropriately. Savor the feeling of success when the interview concludes on a positive note. Replay this mental videotape several times each day, particularly before falling asleep every night and while exercising. These are the times when your mind is most relaxed and receptive to positive programming. As Henry Ford once said, "Think you can, think you can't—either way you're right." Build your self-confidence by convincing yourself that you will succeed.

Figure 7.3 provides an **Interview Feedback Sheet** for you to use in rehearsing your interview. Get a colleague or someone else (possibly a friend or family member) to work with you, and role play the interview using a video camera. My résumé and interview students are always surprised at how they look on video. They notice little flaws that they never thought about before. And they are always amazed at how much they improve with practice. If you don't own a video camera, rent one from your local camera shop—it will be a worthwhile investment to see yourself in action. Critiquing the tape with your partner will allow you to identify your weaknesses and make changes to create the image you want at every level: appearance, body language, voice control, and information.

To write your video script, you can prepare interviewer questions based on what you've recorded in Figures 7.1 and 7.2. You can also script questions for yourself to ask the interviewer, based on your research notes regarding the job and company. You can use the section in this chapter on Handling Questions to get ideas for scripting tough questions that the interviewer will ask you, then prepare your responses.

Words From The Wise

Murphy's Law says that, no matter how well prepared you are for a great interview, whatever can go wrong will. Careful planning is the best way to counter this.

I recommend calling the department secretary or receptionist to

INTERVIEW FEEDBACK SHEET

Nonverbal

Evaluate your interviews in terms of advice given in this section on the following areas of nonverbal communication. Write OK if interviewee follows the advice. If they don't follow the advice, indicate what needs to be corrected.

Appearance	*Interview #1*	*Interview #2*
• color and cut of clothing • hairstyle • jewelry • makeup • nail polish • shoes and stockings • briefcase • glasses		
Body Language and Other Nonverbal Cues	*Interview #1*	*Interview #2*
• demeanor • carriage • eye contact • gestures • facial expression • nervous habits • tilting the head • nervous laughter • tone of voice • clarity of speech • language • rate of speech • humor • energy • enthusiasm • listening		

Verbal
Did the candidate project power and self confidence? Interview #1 Interview #2
Did the candidate answer the tough questions in such a way as to convince the employer of his or her competence and value to the organization? Interview #1 Interview #2
Did the candidate demonstrate knowledge of the company and its products or services? Interview #1 Interview #2
Did the candidate "interview" the employer by asking intelligent questions about the job, why position is open, level of responsibility, reporting relationship, department goals? Interview #1 Interview #2

Figure 7.3
Make copies of this sheet to record your interview feedback. Then file in your Job Search Notebook under section 7.

confirm your appointment the day before the interview and verifying details such as:

- any security procedures
- exact location
- parking arrangements
- number of people interviewing you
- names and titles of those interviewing you

It's worthwhile to make a trip over to the office as a trial run. This will give you a chance to calculate how long it takes to get there from home. Remember to add a few extra minutes if you'll be traveling during rush hour. Figure out where you'll park, and which entrance you'll use. If it's a secured facility, make sure you find out what the procedure is for applicants. It's difficult to be relaxed in the interview when you've dealt with several frustrations on the way over.

If possible, go up to the office you'll be visiting (if you haven't already done such research). This will give you a chance to get some excellent clues as to their dress expectations and company culture, which will be quite helpful in your interview. Having been through a dry run like this will help calm butterflies on the day of the interview.

When the day arrives, you can prevent Murphy's Law from proving itself by taking such simple preventive measures as allowing plenty of extra time for everything, getting plenty of rest the night before, and having a good meal or nutritious snack before leaving home! Many people make the mistake of thinking they can't eat before the interview because they're too nervous. Then, in the interview, their blood sugar drops and fatigue sets in, using up all the energy and enthusiasm they need to get the job.

Managers in every industry have pet peeves about interviews. I have seen and heard plenty of horror stories. Here are the top ten dislikes of interviewers (in no special order):

1. lack of focus and direction: job hopping
2. no self-confidence, too timid
3. conceited, self-centered, arrogant
4. too much emphasis on pay, benefits, advancement
5. not well-organized, uncertain
6. didn't answer the questions, rambled
7. dressed too casually

8. didn't show interest in department or company

9. seemed nervous, stiff, and formal; no energy

10. lacked enthusiasm for the job

Conversely, all managers have their favorite interview qualities. Here are some of my favorites and others that managers from different industries have shared with me (in no special order).

1. clear, concise answers
2. an interest in making a contribution
3. enthusiasm
4. knowledge of our company and products
5. self-confidence
6. relaxed demeanor
7. sense of humor
8. promptness
9. appropriate dress and grooming
10. sense of direction in career

I'm often asked about how to bring up salary, benefits, and other concerns. These are all issues that should be discussed after the offer is made. In most industries, applicants for positions above entry level are required to go through at least two interviews.

In tough times, it's best to wait until they make you an offer to ask about salary, vacation, travel, overtime policies, and benefits. Then if these points aren't suitable, you can refuse the offer or negotiate more favorable terms. Your contributions, what you have to offer, should be the focus of your interviews because your purpose is to get the job. Once you know that they want you, you're in a much better bargaining position.

If the interviewer specifies salary or benefits in the interview and asks you if they're acceptable, you can always say you'd like to think about it and negotiate later. If you decide that you don't like their offer, you can always say you got a better one elsewhere.

In my résumé and interview workshops, participants often ask about the following issues:

What if the interviewer offers you a cigarette, food or drink?

A simple "no thank you" is the best response. If you proclaim that you don't smoke, this could be interpreted to mean that you're vehemently opposed to those who do. And, if your interviewer smokes, your response could be a strike against you. Of course, you should never light up in an interview.

It's probably a good idea to refuse any food or drink offered to you in the interview. A jittery coffee cup or embarrassing cake crumbs are just more details to worry about when you want to concentrate on your presentation. If you have dry mouth or a sore throat, it's a good idea to carry mints or lozenges in your pocket. Explain that you have a sore throat before putting them in your mouth. This is better than choking on your words, and you'll feel more relaxed.

What should I bring to the interview?

As I mentioned earlier, I prefer the sleek, unencumbered look of a simple leather portfolio. Inside, there's room for everything you'll need: pen and paper in case you want to make a note of anything, a calendar, extra copies of your résumé, a few samples of your work, selected recommendations, and miscellaneous items, such as a calculator. It's also a good idea to take a copy of the company's annual report or product literature to peruse while you wait. Having this in hand as you make your entrance will show enthusiasm for the company.

Never bring food or gifts for the interviewer. I once interviewed a bright young man for a development advisor position at a large manufacturing and design firm who brought leftover Chinese food for my director, who was interviewing him after me. I'm sure he meant well, but the gesture was risky (especially since he'd kept the food in his hotel room, unrefrigerated, overnight!). He was not invited back by the director for a second interview.

What attire do you recommend for a recent grad on a tight budget?

Shopping for an important event on a budget requires skill and creativity. Here are some guidelines that will help you get the most from your dollars.

Remember that you'll be seated during most of the interview and you'll want to focus the attention on your face. With this in mind, it makes sense to emphasize the upper body with a light colored shirt or jacket. A good-looking jacket is a must. A good haircut is also a worthwhile investment. For women, quality jewelry, such as simple earrings and a necklace, will help to draw attention to the face. For men, a necktie serves this purpose. (Earrings for men are still a risk in most businesses.) A good-looking dark skirt or trousers and shoes can be purchased inexpensively; dark colors don't show detail and fabric quality as well as lighter colors do. The eye will be drawn upward toward your lighter-colored shirt or jacket.

Can you give me any tips for composing myself before answering tough interview questions?

One simple (and fun) technique that I recommend to my interview students seems to work well. In the days before the interview, pay attention to how a public figure you admire handles tough questions or sensitive issues. Analyze the person's technique and try to emulate it. When you're in the interview and a tough question comes up, ask yourself, "How would the president or prime minister handle this?" Then pretend you're that person and carry on with your role play. It's fun, and it will help you to relax and actually enjoy the interview.

Some people say you should make conversation with the receptionist before the interview in order to make a positive impression. Should I do this?

Yes. I've seen cases where applicants who impressed the receptionist with intelligent questions and enthusiasm about the company won the job when the chips were down.

It's a well-known fact in business that many sharp receptionists and secretaries have their boss's ears. A smart manager will listen carefully to the observations of a perceptive subordinate who is skilled at evaluating visitors. I've seen a director and a vice-president of one major corporation go out to the lobby after interviewing to ask the receptionist what she thought.

Whether or not you have a conversation with the receptionist, it pays to be pleasant, polite, and respectful to everyone. One receptionist at a small law firm told me that when she once asked an applicant the purpose of his visit, he said it was none of her business and that as far as she was concerned, he could be here to sell the interviewer pantyhose! When she announced the applicant, that is exactly what she told her boss—that the applicant was there to sell pantyhose. This is an extreme case, but it does illustrate how rudeness and arrogance will certainly work against you.

What's the best way to handle illegal questions regarding such things as age, marital status, and children?

This is difficult for most people. It seems like a Catch-22, because even though you're reluctant to reveal personal information, you don't want to seem uncooperative and lose your chance at the job. In such cases, I advise turning the focus back to the job, as I mentioned earlier in this chapter. Ask if this factor (age, marriage, family) is a requirement of the job. Immediately follow this rhetorical question with support to show that this factor has never affected your performance in the past. Stress that you've always been able to work regular hours, overtime when needed, travel, or whatever you think the issues might be.

I was once hired for a professional position when I was five months pregnant. When I was asked about my condition, I explained that I wasn't planning to take any time off. (And I didn't need to, because my son was very cooperative, and was born during Christmas break. I was able to work until my due date and return at the beginning of the new year!)

How do you weave your recommendations and work samples into the interview?

This requires judgment. There's no set formula; it's a matter of timing. You might choose to wait until you're discussing performance and special achievements, and then say something like, "By the way, I brought a few samples/recommendations with me. Would you like to see them?" It's better to share them one at a time. You don't want the interviewer to feel that you're overdoing it. At the end of the interview, you can always offer to leave anything you didn't get a chance to discuss.

Recommendations and work samples are a strategy that most of your competitors probably won't use unless these items are requested, so this is another good way to set yourself apart.

How can I tell if the interview is going well?

Your sense of the interaction is primarily based on gut feel. However, there are a few observations you can make to check your interview status. First of all, how do you feel? If you've prepared a great script and rehearsed well, you should be feeling relaxed and confident. When this is the case, the interview will most likely be going well. Second, evaluate the interviewer's reaction Of course, it's difficult to read a person you've just met, and you need to make allowances for differences in style. For example, some people are naturally more warm and friendly than others. But go ahead and ask yourself these questions: Are you in sync with him or her? Does the interviewer seem to be relaxing and enjoying the interview? Is he or she acting warm and friendly toward you? If you've answered yes to all of these, the interview is probably going well.

INTERVIEW FOLLOW-UP

There is one final challenge for you to handle in the week following your interview. It's important to follow up your interview with a short letter reinforcing your interest in the position and the company.

Whether they've already made the decision to hire you or if your application is still under consideration, this will strengthen their impression of you as a thorough professional and will serve to reestablish contact with the employer.

Like the cover letter, the follow-up letter should be short and focused on what you can do for the employer. Figure 7.4 provides an excellent model for this.

Your letter should include cover the following basic components:

Opening Paragraph – Thank the employer for the interview referencing the position you're applying for and the day or date of your interview.

Middle Paragraph(s) – Reemphasize your enthusiasm for the position and the company. Using the new information you got in the interview, tailor your potential contributions to department priorities and problem solving. Highlight any special qualifications that may have been overlooked in the interview. If discussed in the interview, you may want to send additional information (such as recommendations or work samples) at this time.

Closing Paragraph – Refer to the next step, such as additional interviews, by saying that you'll call the department secretary to set up your next interview as discussed or, if appropriate, you'll wait for them to call you. Most companies require second or third interviews for positions higher than entry level.

The techniques you have learned in this chapter will enable you to project the power and self-confidence you need to clinch the job that's just right for you.

125 Pinecrest Drive
Anywhere, USA 12345

February 14, 19__

Mr. Joe Blank
TVS Incorporated
Anywhere, USA 12345

Dear Mr. Blank:

thank the interviewer and reference day of interview

Thank you for the interesting interview last Monday morning. I talked with Jim and John for about 90 minutes after you left and have thought about the position on your staff ever since.

tailored contribution

At first I was primarily interested in joining your staff because of the opportunity to work as assistant producer on a prime-time talk show. After talking with Jim and John, I began to understand your department priorities in more detail. In particular, I was struck by the amount of work you have facing you and the lack of administrative and organizational resources. (Having used a computer for the last five years, I could not begin to design a program without a word processing program at my fingertips, yet your group has only one computer to share, and marginal administrative support on top of that!)

enthusiasm for job

It seems that I could assist you in several ways. First, as we discussed, I am an experienced producer and program developer. Second, I have a well-rounded background in computers and could assist you and your staff in automating some of the more tedious administrative duties. This could involve training interested members of the professional staff in word processing skills or spreadsheets, which, once learned, would greatly reduce their work load and their frustration concerning lack of administrative support. Lastly, I would be very interested in working directly with your administrative staff in designing a more job-enriching and motivating environment for them. I started my work life as a secretary and feel that I have first-hand understanding of the frustrations involved in that type of work.

refers to next step — Thank you again for the interview. Please also thank Jim and John for taking so much time out of their schedules to speak with me. I'll call you next week to check on the status of my application.

Sincerely,

Maureen Smith

page 2 of 2

Figure 7.4: Sample of strong follow up letter

As you complete the chapter on how to have a great interview, you should have prepared and filed the following documents in your **Job Search Notebook** under the Interview section.

Self Description

List of Stories, Weaknesses, and Support

Findings on Research of Company and Job

Achievements Presentation Planning Sheet

Interview Feedback Sheet

CHAPTER 8

Getting your Foot in the Door: An Alternative for Tough Times

"Happiness is the exercise of one's vital abilities along lines of excellence in a life that affords them scope..."

—*Anonymous Greek*

With the 1990s service and information economy comes a burgeoning market for consultant services in every industry. The information explosion and popular human potential philosophy have created high demand for basic information and self-improvement programs in every field. This translates to a plethora of entrepreneurial opportunities for anyone with any degree of specialized knowledge. Here are some examples of such areas:

Possible Consultant Opportunities	
investment	travel consultant
real estate	teaching English as a second language
foreign language	consumer issues
image consulting	communication skills
presentation skills	self-defense
time management	résumé preparation
personal organization	fitness
taxes/accounting	nutrition
word processing	personal shopping
computers	managing work teams
interior decorating	organizing events
health care	study skills
hazardous waste	

If you've identified a corporate position as your career goal but are having difficulty finding the right corporate job in tough times, consulting can be an excellent alternative to help you get your foot in the door for a future corporate job. Larry used this strategy successfully when he became a consultant on effective presentations for corporations. In tough times, many companies are understaffed and don't have the budget to hire full-time specialists for this type of training. Paradoxically, at the same time it's crucial for staff members who do sales presentations to have top notch presentation skills to bring in new business. The solution for many companies is to bring in a consultant to provide what's needed on a temporary basis. Larry was hired by a large public relations firm to teach effective presentations. They liked his work and, after a few months, when the hiring freeze was lifted, they hired Larry as a permanent employee.

Consulting can also help broaden your skills when you're leaving a company job to prepare for a new, higher-level position within the corporate ranks.

Marla, a former airline stewardess turned consultant, has built a successful business teaching people about in-flight safety and crash survival techniques. Carl is another good example. While working as a representative at a government protection agency, he realized that most small companies are confused about the myriad of ever-changing laws which regulates hazardous chemicals. And because most small companies are not sure how to get the information they need, Carl saw an opportunity to help them interpret hazardous chemical regulations. He left the agency and set up a very successful business consulting with small companies.

The information explosion has created an age of opportunity for creative career planners. There are more options today than at any other time in history. Creativity, self-knowledge, and goal setting will help you discover new career possibilities and invent career niches for you in the information economy.

Use the **Possible Consultant Opportunities List** as a model for building your own list of possibilities. Brainstorm! Be creative and list as many as you can think of—even if they seem unrealistic at the time. Once you've created a long list, you can file it in your Job Search Notebook under section 8 and go back later to prioritize based on what you think would work best for you.

Multidimensional careers are an excellent strategy for tough times. Your alternative job can later provide you with a safety net, just in case the bottom falls out of your core career, as we've seen happen in so many industries recently. Developing a sideline is a good way to protect yourself against inflation as well as possible cutbacks in your industry.

In choosing an area for consulting, it's important to make sure that your choice is clearly related to your core career, so that it seems like a natural outgrowth rather than a diversion. Deviating too far from your chosen career can make you seem scattered or indecisive to future employers. You should be sure that consulting experience will be seen as a way of building and adding to your career skills rather than a money-making stopgap.

For example, Marianne, an out of work graphic artist, developed a consulting business in the field of home decorating. This experience broadened her background and enhanced her qualifications for a future job with the home furnishing section of a major department store. Her consulting also helped her develop valuable contacts in the industry. If Marianne had decided to go into real estate investment consulting instead, her consulting experience would probably work against her when applying for another artist job.

The key to using consulting as a successful strategy is to refer back to your career goals established in Chapter 1 and select a field that fits in with your goals.

If you've decided to switch careers, consulting, side line jobs, and free-lance work are excellent ways to develop the experience you'll need to get your foot in the door of your new career. High energy people often develop a sideline or do free-lance work for this reason (also as a source of extra income). If your extra work is related to your current career, it will add to your credentials, which can speed you along toward your career goals. If it's unrelated, it will help you to build an experience base for your new career. In either case, consulting, sideline, or free-lance work should be focused on your career goals established in Chapter 1. William James, the renowned American psychologist, had excellent advice on this: "Wish then for one thing exclusively and not for a hundred other incompatible things just as strongly."

The key is to establish your goals and galvanize your talent, energy, and determination around those goals. Giving your attention to anything else is dissipating your resources.

As you complete this chapter and analyze your alternatives for tough times, you should have filed the following list in your **Job Search Notebook** under section 8, Possible Consultant Opportunities.

Possible Consultant Opportunities

Epilogue

Your mission to land the job you want in tough times has been accomplished. If you've followed the advice in this book, you've sold yourself as the perfect candidate for the job. Your self-confident, energetic presentation at the interview was supported with specific detail about your skills and experience, and the way you turned even the toughest questions into another opportunity to highlight your strengths really clinched the job for you.

By methodically following the systematic plan you designed for yourself—from laying the groundwork with your career goals to creating your unique self-marketing package—you followed through with discipline and perseverance to get the job you wanted.

More than anything, success in the job market requires diligence and patience. Ray Kroc, who built McDonald's from a simple malt shop into a phenomenally successful fast-food chain, said it best in his autobiography, Grinding It Out: "Press on! Nothing in the world can take the place of persistence. Talent will not; nothing is more common than unsuccessful individuals with talent. Genius will not; the world is full of educated derelicts. Persistence and determination alone are omnipotent."

Suggested Readings

Anthony, Robert. *Total Self Confidence*. New York: Berkley Books, 1979.

Brothers, Joyce. *How to Get Whatever You Want Out of Life*. New York: Ballantine Books, 1987.

Brothers, Joyce. *The Successful Woman*. New York: Ballantine Books, 1980.

Cassedy, Ellen and Nussbaum, Karen. *9 to 5: The Working Woman's Guide to Office Survival*. New York: Penguin Books, 1983.

Dyer, Wayne W. *The Sky's the Limit*. New York, Pocket Books, 1980.

Foxworth, Jo. *Burn Out*. New York: Warner Books, 1978.

Harragan, Betty Lehan. *Games Mother Never Taught You: Corporate Gamesmanship For Women*. New York: Warner Books, 1977.

Naisbitt, John. *Megatrends*. New York: Warner Books, 1984.

Noe, John R. *Peak Performance for High Achievers*. New York: Berkeley Books, 1984.

Molloy, John T. *Live for Success*. New York: Bantam Books, 1981.

Molloy, John T. *The Women's Dress for Success Book*. New York: Warner Books, 1977.

Toffler, Alvin. *The Third Wave*. Toronto: Bantam Books, 1980.

Wyse, Lois. *The Six-Figure Woman/and How to Be One*. New York: Fawcett Crest, 1983.

About The Author

Julianne Fowler, M.A., manages professional development at a Fortune 100 corporation in Los Angeles. She teaches graduate business courses at UCLA and USC. She also consults and conducts productivity workshops for organizational clients including the City of Los Angeles, Kennedy Space Center, the National Management Association, and *The Daily News*. She lives in Los Angeles with her attorney husband and two children. Ms. Fowler is currently working on her second book, *Managing Transitions in Business and Life*.